Stories are Medicine

Stories are Medicine:

Writing to Heal

AN ANTHOLOGY

Edited by Gina L. Carroll

STORY HOUSE TX
Houston

ISBN: 979-8-9858303-0-9

PUBLISHED IN THE UNITED STATES
by Story House TX, Houston, Texas.

Disclaimer: Although Story House TX (the Publisher) has made every effort to ensure that the information in this book was correct as submitted by the contributors at press time, the Publisher does not assume and hereby disclaims any liability to any party for any loss, damage, or disruption caused by errors or omissions, whether such errors or omissions result from negligence, accident, or any other cause. Each named author whose story is included in this book (Contributor) retains the full rights of ownership and copyright; takes full responsibility for the content of her story; and has represented to Publisher that the facts contained in the stories are true. Each Contributor has set forth the facts of her story as best as she remembers them, without intent to harm or negatively impact anyone. They recognize their memories of the events described in their stories may be experienced and/or remembered differently than other persons mentioned therein.

Contributor credits begin on page 117

Frontispiece by Danielle Boodoo-Fortune
design by deborah daly

Contents

"When you write in your own voice,
you become subject rather than object.
You transform your own destiny."

—bell hooks

(RIP - September 25, 1952 – December 15, 2021)

Foreword

The *Stories Are Medicine* workshop was inspired by a group of women that I had the pleasure of leading through an eight-week course entitled, *Use Your Medicine, Woman.* The course explored the idea that we all come into the world with medicine inside of us in the form of our gifts, our wisdom, our dreams, our words, and yes, our stories and so much more. Our medicine contributes to our healing, first for ourselves, and then for others as it emanates from us out into the world. Each week, we gathered online in what we called a sacred container, a safe space, one that was not recorded in order to encourage vulnerability and freedom. The participants poured out their hearts to women who were, at first, strangers, new faces in a ZOOM square, but who eventually became friends with a beautiful bond.

As a women's ministry leader for twenty-five years, I've always been amazed how the people I'm called to serve somehow make me a better leader. They inspire me as I watch them shift and transform. It's like an energy exchange. As I give and pour out my own medicine, I experience healing in return from the very ones I lead. And that's what happened with this course and this group of resilient women. The more they shared themselves by sharing their stories, the more inspired I became. My role was to simply guide them and hold space for their healing, but I too, found healing in their stories. After I ended the class each week, I felt energized, purpose-filled and ready for the next week. By week eight, I didn't want the experience to end, so I offered them an opportunity to share their medicine in the community by meeting regularly. Because of our busy schedules, we were not always able to meet, but I knew some of them had some pretty amazing stories that the world needed to hear.

So I reached out to my dear friend, Gina Carroll, who helped edit my first two books. I knew she was forming writing groups with her company, Story House, and was bringing people together to tell their stories. I asked her if we could form a Stories Are Medicine writing group and publish these stories in an anthology. A couple of the ladies joined us from the *Use Your Medicine, Woman* course, and we recruited others who were ready to share their medicine with the world. Gina was the leader this time. We met weekly, and over the course of ten weeks, Gina guided us on a journey of discovering our most pressing story, finding our theme and illustration, and getting the story out of us and onto the page. My favorite part of this experience was listening to each woman share her story and receiving feedback from the group. We bonded over our stories, and got to know each other even better. Not only did we find our voices, but we also found our medicine in each word as we read the drafts out loud over and over, first to ourselves and then to the group.

It is our intention that as you read these beautiful stories, you too will be inspired to share the healing medicine of your own.

—Kimberly Bady

Preface

When I think about the one story process, I am reminded of the scene in the movie, *Ghost,* when Whoopi Goldberg's character, Oda Mae, finally comes into her psychic abilities. Before this moment, she is a lightweight con artist taking advantage of people's beliefs and taking their money by pretending to summon their deceased loved ones. But now that she has actually been visited upon by a real ghost, Patrick Swayze's character, Sam, she suddenly hears the voices of all manner of spirits from beyond, all crowding her tiny séance room, attempting to speak to the living. When one customer sits at Oda Mae's table, the room is full of the expectant customer's family ghosts, fighting for the chance to be heard. Oda Mae is literally jumped by a spirit impatient for an audience. It's a hilarious moment where Oda Mae is overwhelmed and overwrought, so much so, that she orders "everybody OUT," banishing people and spirits alike.

This is how it feels in my head when I am trying to settle upon one among my many stories clamoring to be written. How in the world do I choose just one? How might I narrow down the field when they are all loud and demanding to be told? And once I choose the most pressing story, how do I quiet the others in order to fully focus on the one?

The answer is that once you settle on one story, the clamor quiets and your focus sharpens. And once the one most pressing story is extracted, dissected and told fully with precision, it makes room in your head for the others to stretch their arms and stand in line, confident that they will be told as well.

The writers whose stories you will find in these pages have done something monumental. They came together, seeking to answer the clamoring going on in their heads. They made the tough decisions about which pressing stories to tell. And then, each took the brave steps to examine that story for the meaning and truths that promised to heal. They toiled and grappled and wrangled. They chiseled their stories into solid works of art. They transformed them from clamoring thoughts to real, physical things. And then, they took that final courageous step and released their words, confident that someone else could be, would be, helped and healed, too.

And so, in a very real and tangible sense, this book and these stories are offerings—a reminder that we are all a part of something big, that our stories can be the same and different at the same time, and in so being, they bind us together so that we can heal ourselves and each other.

Our stories are medicine. We are medicine women. We can own our words, minister to our own healing, *and* we can give them away as the prescription someone didn't even know they needed. We can tell one story and then release it with the full knowledge that *that* one story does not define us. And when we release that one story, we have readied ourselves to write the next.

Take these stories as the gifts that they are, and when you have consumed them fully, take your own steps, claim your own place in the storytelling universe and begin.

—Gina L. Carroll
Editor

Carla —
Be a seed bearer of wisdom.
106-2022

We Are Seeds

INGE FORD

"They tried to bury us,

but they did not know we were seeds."

—DINOS CHRISTIANOPOLOUS

In West Africa, the Songhai (Songhay) Empire laid at the crossroads of trade routes leading both to North Africa and Egypt to the east. Information and multi-cultural exchange were commonplace among travelers roving these routes. This demographic revered her elders. The Songhai were known as fearless warriors, multi-talented people, flush with highly organized communities that included agro-fishermen, artisans, griots, writers, and free commoners. Elders were considered the custodians of sage wisdom, generosity, and grace. An obligation of elders was to impart, with dignity, worldly knowledge to generations. This still stands true today. From Africa to the southern shores of the United States, elders are those ripened with experience and respect, and are reservoirs of old words.

Thirty miles outside of Shreveport, Louisiana, exists a small town called Minden. My great-Nana's home is there. It's the summer of 1970. It's July and hot as Hades. Skies are cloudless and blue. The fragrance of Confederate jasmine blossoms gently wafts through the warm breeze. I know it is going to be a scorcher because the timber of cicadas is almost deafening. Did you know that male cicadas use their tymbal membranes to make clicking sounds to attract mates? Their sound is amplified when the weather is hot.

It's Saturday morning and the tinny sounding transistor radio is blaring, "Magic 102.9, Classic Soul in Shreveport, Louisiana." The song, *Ball of Confusion*, by The Temptations, is playing ...

Well the only person talking about
love thy brother is the Preacher
And its seems nobody's interested in learning
but the Teacher
Segregation, determination, demonstration, integration
Aggravation, humiliation, obligation to our nation
Ball of confusion
Oh yeah, that's what the world is today...
woo hey...
...Oh great googa-looga, can't you hear me talking to
you
Just a ball of confusion

Oh yeah, that's what the world is today
Hey, hey…

"In'gah, come help me get this laundry on the line," Nana calls from behind the bedroom door.

"Yes, Ma'am. I'm coming," I respond.

I love my great-grandmother because she asks so little of us, lives simply, and seems to me to be a bona fide balance between the mortal and mystic planes of the universe.

I jump from the metal frame bed that seems almost five feet above the ground. I quickly put on my cutoff denim shorts, tank top, and my newly delivered, catalog-ordered pair of Montgomery Ward's wooden clogs. With moderate haste, I scurry through Nana's small bungalow: 606 Walnut Street is a well-appointed space—two bedrooms and one bath. The house is set on cinder block pilings and furnished with many places to 'sit a spell,' a solid wood wardrobe in the living room, Nana's big Lazy-Boy chair, and a dusty black & white television adorned with a foil tipped rabbit-ear antenna. I make my way through the kitchen and grab off the table a handful of freshly picked blackberries that my sister and I gathered along the railroad tracks the day before. Then I navigate my way around the behemoth vintage wringer washer machine (circa 1950s) to scoop up the laundry Nana had wrung. As I emerge from the back porch with a white enamel bucket, heavy with garments, my eyes meet my great-grandmothers' and I smile.

My maternal great-grandmother, a.k.a. Nana, was a soft spoken yet commanding vessel of feminine and masculine energy. The best we could learn was that Nana was a progeny of a band of Black Freedman Cherokee Indians and enslaved survivors of the diaspora. She was a seeker, traveler, builder, and a matron of a Pentecostal church. She was a medicine woman, seamstress, quilter, gardener, cook, cantor, chronicler, an avid reader of the Bible and the local newspaper. This elder stood nearly six feet tall. She had a wingspan that commanded attention. When she was feeling jubilant in church, or enjoying television troubadours like Engelbert Humperdinck and Tom Jones, her large strong hands would collide and resound like a thunderclap. While in her forties, my Nana's smooth dark skin was afflicted with vitiligo, a condition that causes loss of pigmentation and skin blotches. While this auto-immune condition was all over her physical frame, it did not affect the radiant twinkle in her eyes nor the delight of her smile.

My sister, four years my junior, and I, were afforded extended excursions to Minden during summer breaks. As unaccompanied minors, we traveled via Greyhound Bus Lines from Houston, Texas. The reason for our visits, whether purely for the city-country experience, or to get out of our parents' hair, was of little consequence to me. I got to be the big sister—large and in charge, the protector and keeper of the vittles. Nourishment for the long nine-hour haul consisted of fried chicken, homemade biscuits, slices of pound cake and tea cakes, fresh fruit—usually fresh cut oranges or watermelon, and our mother's tart yet sweet lemonade, chilling in a heavy stainless steel thermos. Mom neatly wrapped each item with waxed paper secured in tin foil and included two clean tea towels. All of this was hand packed in a large, doubled paper grocery bag. My younger sister was always claiming to be hungry, but as the "elder" watchman, it was my duty to make sure that our provisions lasted the duration of our journey. After all, I was becoming a pro at this pilgrimage, as this was our third summer of traveling unchaperoned.

During our visits to Louisiana, my sister, E.J. and I made friends with the neighborhood kids, a ragtag mix of females and males around our age, who seemed to us to have had total freedom to explore this small town and all of its nooks and crannies. Through them, we quickly learned what "be home before the streetlights come on" meant.

This summer, once everyone›s daily chores are done, the goofy ganglet of approximately eight to ten pubescent bodies gather in my Nana's front yard around noon, as was the practice on most weekdays and Saturdays. We travel by foot to the community swimming pool which is about one and half miles away. We are a feral pack of tween-agers donned in swimsuits under our clothes, outgrown sneakers with the toes cut out to make sandals, a towel, and fifty cents. There are no sunglasses, sunblock, protective floaties, nose clips, eye goggles, or other modern accoutrements for a day out in sweltering temperatures of more than ninety degrees. The pool entry fee is twenty-five cents—a bargain for a day of splish-splashing in a highly chlorinated cement pond. Taking the long route home is usually a given. The diversion includes a pass by "Miss B's" converted garage walk-up-stand for various five to ten cent treats—i.e. moon cookies, jumbo dill or sour pickles, peppermint sticks, Kool-Aid pops or whatever concoctions Miss B has conjured today.

As city girls, my sister and I are novelties to our kin. We dress slightly differently. My Louisiana sisters hot comb and press their hair with Dixie Peach pomade. My sister and I wear afros and plaits. Our mom makes sure her girls are groomed. Our clothes, while not expensive, are in good repair, colorful and coordinated. I have a new swimsuit this year. My first moonblood came in the spring before our summer visit with Nana, just shy of my 13th birthday. I overhear Mom on the phone telling Nana that she'd send ample feminine protection for me and extra money, if needed.

"Nana, Inge gets very excited about her period. She hasn't complained about any pain or moodiness.

We're trying to make sure she understands the importance of keeping up her personal hygiene," Mom said.

Well, I must look pretty good in my new modest two-piece swimsuit on this Thursday in July, because He buys me six moon cookies—they are only a penny each—plus an infamous Miss B's "love nest" soft serve confection. Just for me. He is almost fifteen years old. He is a tall and lanky piece of chocolate with a wide front-tooth gap, a low 'fro and that freshly deepened bass to his voice that adolescence bestows. The gang takes quick notice as He and I slow our pace while walking home from the pool. I feel celebrated and flattered. When I get back to Walnut Street, I tell my Nana about the day.

"I think he likes me," I say in a tickled voice.

"Umph," Nana scoffs.

The chickens and ducklings are super active this Saturday morning. Nana and I hang the laundry as if we are on an assembly line. She places the items on cords of tightly wound hemp and places the garments just as she wants. I follow behind, binding them with wooden clothespins.

"In'gah, prop the pole in dat hole and push the line up," she commands.

"Yes, ma'am," I reply, and diligently do what is ordered.

Four long lines of sheets, towels, shirts, pants, brassieres, panties, opaque stockings all sway with the summer breeze. Nana and I engage in light conversation about what we will have for supper and there is confirmation of a blackberry cobbler for dessert. I proceed to prop each clothesline higher in alternate holes.

And then with no warning, she says, "In'gah, the hole outlasts the pole."

"Huh? Okay. Yes, Ma'am," I chuckle with a confused expression on my face.

Nana, with smiling eyes, pauses, looks me square in my face with calm resolve then turns to place more clothes on the line. She says that my mother told her about me having started my moon cycle. She reminds me that I must be mindful of my hygiene. She speaks of elder remedies and healing practices that I can adopt should I have discomfort before, during, or after my cycle. She authorizes and gives me agency to bask in the divine power I possess and will experience each month. She, with few words and gentle intonation, requests that I be mindful when I engage with a "worthy right-mate." She directs me to learn how to listen and honor my spirit.

"All interests ain't worthy," Nana laments.

I share the events of that great summer with my mother upon my return to Houston. My mom laughs when I mention the clothesline incident. But there is no clarification.

My summer retreats to Minden dwindled after

I turned fourteen-years-old. High school activities, summer enrichment camps, and travel opportunities became a priority. I continued to regularly communicate with my Nana with cards, letters and phone calls. The precious notes from her with commentary on how to right my ship, a timely passage from the Bible, or the unforgettable enclosed "pieces of money" (usually a dollar or two or a $2 bill) always brought joy upon receipt. I visited her regularly with my own children until her death at one-hundred-and-three-years-old.

Several years after my last summer in Louisiana, I was attending college. I was in a long-term romantic relationship with a slightly older mate. The relationship seemed to have run its course. One evening, our amorous plans were dashed as he struggled with his sexual prowess. Disappointed, I turned onto my side to fall asleep that night. I began to breathe slowly and reassess my dissatisfaction with the whole situation, almost wanting to sob. All kinds of thoughts were running through my head. Then, with little provocation, I began to giggle, quietly, not trying to be disrespectful. Nana's ah-ha wisdom bubbled up inside me,..."the HOLE outlasts the POLE." Wait! What? Great googa-looga, can't you hear me talking to ya...MY ball of confusion just made some prolific sense.

My elder, my great-Nana knew the circle of life. She was guiding me toward a path to follow and passing on worldly knowledge. A woman's powerful capacity to receive and to bring forth life is a blessing that deserves respect; not only by the vessel holder but by those allowed to enter the fold. She was educating me about the ecstasy that can be experienced between men and women. And about the divine feminine. She was telling me about the importance of healing, the despair of suffering. She laid knowledge tracks of purpose and connection from the past to the present to the future. My elder, unknowingly to me then, shared an existential reason, and in a joyful, dignified manner, made me a reservoir, a seed bearer of old words.

The Bittersweet Goodbye

Kimberly Bady

"At the end of life, what matters most is not what we bought, but what we built; not what we got, but what we shared; not our competence, but our character; and not our success, but our significance..." —Anonymous

It had been four months of weekly visits with my father, who had been diagnosed with stage four lymphoma. This particular visit to the MD Anderson Cancer Center would be very different from any other.

As usual, I was prepared to stay a while. Usually sitting for hours to relieve family members who had been there earlier in order for them to take a break, a walk, get something to eat, or go home to change clothes and rest. However, on this day, I was only there for less than 10 minutes. I walked into the room, and to my surprise, Dad was sitting up and talking. I smiled, so grateful that he was back in the hospital. He surely had not looked this vibrant yesterday, when I visited him at his home in the country.

Maybe we still have more time with him, I thought. Maybe there is a miracle in the making.

Hope sprang up in me even though the doctors had already said there was nothing else they could do. But I looked at my sister's face as she stood next to his bed, seeing her eyes were filled with tears. My brother was standing on the other side of the bed recording from his phone. My stepmother was standing over to the side near the sofa where she slept and her daughters, my step-sisters, were sitting near her.

Then my father began to speak.

"Hey, baby," he said to me as I walked through the door.

"Hey, Daddy," I replied. I held my big smile for him, trying to hide my confusion after reading the room and feeling the weird energy. That was when he began to address me. I was happy he was lucid and seemed to have the strength to sit up and speak, but I was not prepared for what he was about to say.

Just the day before, I had driven the sixty miles from my Houston home to visit him out in the country, Bellville, Texas, where he lived with his wife of twenty-seven years. We never called my stepmother Mom even though she married my dad when we were teenagers. My brother would eventually start calling her Ma'Dea, short for Mother Dear, and then we all did the same, eventually dropping the Ma and just calling her Dea. That seemed like a good compromise. Before then, we called her what everyone else called her in the church my father pastored, Sister Johnson.

Dad didn't look well during that visit in the country. He was in and out of consciousness, sitting in his motorized chair on the porch of their manufactured home. The hospital had already been preparing us for what was to come, hospice care. So as I sat there with my dad, who was slumped over in the chair with labored breathing, I said to Dea, "I think it's time to get hospice involved. They are supposed to keep him comfortable and he doesn't look like he's comfortable. I have a friend who works for a hospice care facility and she gave me some information on a place we can call. I can get the ball rolling now."

Dea was not having it. Perhaps she was not ready for this next step. I could understand that. Perhaps she was holding onto the notion that she could nurse him back to health. Perhaps she took my suggestion personally, as if I were insulting her ability to keep him comfortable. I don't know. But I was very respectful, not trying to override her wishes. I knew she could be very sensitive and fragile, at times. It's not even my personality to force my will. Now, don't get me wrong, I can be fiery and rise to the occasion of the warrior goddess when needed, but not this day.

I was concerned about Dad's discomfort, but I knew I had to choose my words carefully or risk not being allowed to be there with him, at all. Dea had already threatened to limit my sister's visits when she had an issue with Dea, and when my brother asked for some alone time with Dad, Dea told him that she could put him out, too.

I always try to give people the benefit of doubt. Maybe she was overwhelmed at the thought of losing him. Maybe she just wanted everyone to acknowledge that she was a great caregiver. And she was. I won't take that from her. She was by my father's side every step of the way, bathing him, helping him relieve himself since he couldn't walk to the restroom, giving him his medication and feeding him. She did all the things good caregivers do. He had a hip fracture from the weight of a tumor caused by the lymphoma. He was in a lot of pain, so he required constant care, and Dea was his constant care provider. We helped out too, sitting with him and giving her a break when she needed it or had to go to church.

There was always tension when we, his biological children, showed up. My father loved his children and wanted us by his side every day during his illness. He would manage to call us from his flip phone, and if one of the four of us was with him, he was asking where the others were and what time they were coming.

Dea's children, our step siblings, lived nearby, and spent more time with Dad and Dea over the years. So if they were in the room with him when we arrived, they would clear out with an air of resentment. I thought I was imagining it until I overheard my ex-step-sister-in-law tell my brother, one day, that it wasn't fair that we showed up now when Dad was ill when they had been there all along, traveling with him as his ministry team, setting up tent revivals and laboring in camp meetings by his side. Now, we show up, spending this precious time with our father, time they wanted with him.

My intuition was spot on. I felt their disdain beyond the smiles and the small talk, reminding me of my childhood, during the time I lived with Dad. Once my father married Dea and blended our two families, there was never a real blend. It was always them and us, not the Brady Bunch union that onlookers may have seen. As adults, we had our own busy lives and families. My brother pastored his own church. My youngest sister was a staff pastor of a megachurch and my oldest sister and I would go to church occasionally.

By this time, I had distanced myself from my preacher's kid upbringing and former life as a pastor's wife. I was no longer meeting God at church, at the altar or in the pews. I was probably going to yoga on Sundays or communing with God out in nature. Nature was my church - is my church. It's where I feel most connected to the Divine and where God speaks to me.

When Dea and I disagreed about hospice care, it was probably due to the tension of the moment and of our family's history boiling over, after playing nice for months. The thing is—we have never yelled at each other. We did not argue. We did not call names, roll our eyes or throw out any insults. We simply disagreed. I was in my forties, a grown-ass woman with an opinion, and I voiced it. After all, this is what adults do, right? Growing up, though, expressing an opinion or taking a stance was not what we did. But we were not kids anymore. We were no longer living under the same roof with a strict Pentecostal preaching father whom we did not dare defy.

My father made it clear when he married his wife that he expected his children to respect her. And as difficult as that was sometimes, the wrath of my father was far worse. So no backtalking, no eye rolling and no disagreeing, or you would get the belt or tree branch. That was a different day, when my father's generation believed that children best kept their opinions to themselves. This is not quite how many of us raise our children today. At least, not how I've raised my son.

So there I stood in the hospital room, transported to a time decades earlier as a teenager without a voice as my dying father began to speak to me.

In a room full of people, he told me that I had no right to upset his wife with my opinions about his care.

I was being scolded. He had, apparently, scolded my sister before I got there, for her issue with Dea. (I can't remember what my sister's issue was at that time. There were many between them. They never really got along.) Now, it was my turn. I understood ultimately that Dea, his wife and caregiver, had the last say, and I honestly didn't intend to upset her. I had simply watched him on that porch and it had looked as if he were dying right then. I had imagined his transition as a peaceful and sweet goodbye, with him lying in bed surrounded by all of his loved ones, not him falling over in his chair, fighting for every breath until he drew his last one.

This wasn't the first time we'd gotten in trouble for upsetting Dea. There had been many times and she knew just how my father could be. The only discussion we ever had with him to clear things up was the one with the belt.

After he scolded me in the hospital room he said, "I love you and I know you're going to do great things in your life. I believe in you and I'm proud of you." Then he said goodbye.

"I love you, too, Daddy, I said with a shaky voice, tears running down my face. I was overwhelmed with emotions and crying like the little girl who had gotten in trouble. I thought this would be the last time I would see him alive, and that my last memory would be of him chastising me. Again, not the sweet goodbye that I had imagined.

I walked out, wiping the tears from my face. Where were my words? Why didn't I say something? Anything? Why didn't I speak up for myself? I would play that moment in my head over and over for years. But what could I have said? Perhaps, I should have defended my intentions with a brief speech, starting with "Respectfully, Daddy," and ending with, " I love you, too." But I didn't want to cause a scene. I didn't want to upset him further. He was at the end of his life, after all, and in a critical state. I also thought of setting up a meeting with Dea so we could speak like adults and clear things up, but I knew that unless I recorded the conversation, it would backfire, and she would, once again, be the victim who needed saving.

When I left the hospital, I drove to the one place I knew I could find some comfort, my mom's house. Yes, I was that little girl who got in trouble with Dad and wanted nothing but to be comforted by my mommy.

Thankfully, that was not the last time I would see Dad, and unfortunately, that would not be the last instance of drama between *us* and *them*. I had no intention of going back to Dad's house after the hospital incident. I had already said my not-so-sweet goodbye. But he would continue to ask for us daily, so I rode down to the country with my sisters to visit him. Hospice care had been set up by then. He was breathing more easily and more comfortably.

On this particular day, we drove up to the property and approached their mobile home. Dad never got around to fixing up the place. It was a dingy white and falling apart by the day. We drove up the long driveway to the back of the house where everyone parked. I looked around at the cars to assess who was already there. I took a deep breath and set an intention to have a sweet, short visit. When I walked inside, my stepbrother was in the kitchen with his wife and their young child. I said hello and smiled at their little one.

"Don't talk to my family," he said.

"Excuse me?" I said.

He repeated himself and encouraged us, with a string of profanities, to leave or he would "slide us." I stood eye-to-eye with this man, who was known for his violence and run-ins with the police, and who had even physically fought my dad about a year or so earlier, and who, I should mention, had the strength to slide me.

"You can't put me out of my father's house," I said. And I may have thrown a few insults back at him. I may have said, "This isn't your house. Oh yeah, you don't have a house to put anyone out of." My petty side and the warrior goddess in me rose to the occasion, without fear of what he could do to me, to us. My youngest sister quickly called the police and he was made to leave immediately. It was obvious that his mother had given him an earful and he was coming to her defense.

I understood his desire to protect his mother. But I also understood that Dea knew her son's nature and had decided to invoke it toward her end. This was how Dea operated. She was the dutiful wife and First Lady of the church. She would cook for you, bake you a cake. Just don't get on that other side, or she would play the victim and rally her resources to be rescued.

The hurt in my father's eyes after the confrontation still saddens me today. He cried and told us how sorry he was that he could not get out of that bed to protect us from his violent, volatile stepson. We left there thinking this would be our last time in that house. It was just too much drama, too painful. And we didn't expect Dea to allow us to come back.

The next evening one of Dea's daughters called us and asked us to return.

"He's leaving,"' she said, "get here quickly."

We drove as fast as we could to Belleville. When we arrived, we noticed the cars. Others had been called, too and had apparently been there with him all day as he was transitioning. His biological children were the last to be summoned.

We walked into his room and there he was in his bed, slowly drifting off. Eventually, we all gathered around the bed and began to sing. The atmosphere was the most peaceful it had been in months. The lights were dimmed. There were no disagreements, no confrontation. No yelling. No cops were called. No us versus them. It was the sweet goodbye that I had imagined, Dad leaving in a state of peace.

I said goodbye to my father in his physical form that night. But I still feel him with me now. I think of him, and dream of him, often. And I remember that day when he cried because he could not get out of the bed to protect his daughters. Well, now, as an ancestor, He can.

Woman Interrupted

Katherine Johnson

"I didn't get all of my security deposit back... but I got my life."

I still love Atlanta, Georgia. When I moved there, I felt like I was getting a second chance at life. I left my family behind, my four adult children and other loved ones, not knowing the full scope of what was ahead on this new journey. I relocated to Atlanta from Houston, Texas to serve in ministry. The church I attended in Houston had a second location in Atlanta, and I had been invited there to lead praise and worship and work for that ministry. As a former preacher's wife, church elder, minister, ministry leader and choir director, I knew this new assignment required hard work and sacrifice, but I was up for the task, and I was ready for a new start. However, the hopeful opportunity was short-lived. Things didn't work out at the new church. Now, I was in a new city without a job or very much money. I came with my car, and it was in need of repairs, but I just kept on patching it up until I could do better. I was looking for employment and I knew it would come. You might say, I took a big chance and a leap of faith.

After a few weeks, I found a job and a better, friendly, temporary place to live. I really never felt fearful. I knew God had me. I was open to new possibilities, like a nice place to call home, perhaps starting a business, joining a great church, meeting new friends and even finding love, not necessarily in that order.

As I settled in, my family started to visit. We decided to make a trade—they would visit me in Atlanta for Thanksgiving and I would fly home to Texas for Christmas. This was working well. I discovered that my new home had so many great places to eat and so much rich Black history such as the King Center, Dr. King's home and his Church, Ebenezer Baptist Church; a Black mayor; storied HBCU's—and so many world attractions were within my reach. When family visited, I'd show them around to the Coca Cola Factory, the Aquarium, Stone Mountain, and the great shopping within the city and the surrounding areas. As the excited tour guide, I would share what I had learned about the city, such as, did you know the airport is named after Atlanta's first Black mayor, Maynard Jackson, or that so many other civil rights icons lived here, as well? I fell in love with the city. With all its trimmings, Atlanta was like an aphrodisiac. You could find whatever you wanted to soothe your soul. And I met some amazing people who are still my friends to this day.

I found a new job, much different from the one I came for, and I quickly embraced it. Initially, the job required that I live on the work premises of the facility as a Private Care Home Manager of Developmentally Disabled Adults. Later, I was able to live outside the Home in my own residence. I found what I thought was a nice place in Jonesboro, Georgia, close to many amenities, like the grocery stores, the highways, places to eat, a nice mall, the movie theater, etc...and it felt like home.

Often, when I came home from work with groceries or shopping bags, I would see the guy next door, who always seemed to be available to help me carry my packages. Even though I always parked very near my apartment, he seemed to be waiting to "help" me with my things. Although I was open to love, I had already made up my mind that friendship was as far as this relationship would go—nice neighbor, that was it. But he was relentless. He seemed to have already pegged me as a damsel in distress when I was very capable of taking care of myself.

One day, I invited him over to get to know him better. I even invited him to Word of Faith, the amazing church I found and loved. From that first invitation, he was ready every Sunday. I think he even bought a Bible.

Before long, we started enjoying each other's company more and more, developing romantic feelings for one another. Now, my attraction had nothing to do with his status nor what he had in his name, which was nothing. He lived with his nephew and family. He had no car, just a monthly check. There was no real wining or dining, just companionship, which I wanted very much.

As the weeks and months went on, I got an even better job caring for a young man in his home. Sometimes, I would let my new boyfriend drop me off at work so he could use my car. Little by little, he became possessive. He even thought that my employer liked me in a romantic way, and he thought my boss would watch me on cameras installed in his house "for his son's protection." He had quite the imagination. No matter how much I assured him and pleaded with him that none of his accusations were true, he would not believe me. I guess these were the glaring red flags that I ignored.

Still, things progressed in our relationship. He began to stay at my place more than at his own home next door. He asked me to marry him, and I said "yes, in due time." So he went to the jewelry store and bought me an engagement ring. We never did any arguing, but the relationship was not balanced; his passive aggression and covert actions began to take their toll.

After a while, one of my best friends from my hometown of Baltimore, Maryland, came to visit for a few days. I was looking forward to having tons of fun spending time with her, catching up and talking through the night.

When she returned home after our visit, he accused me of being in an intimate relationship with her. His jealousy was really starting to rear its ugly head. How dare he say that about my friend and me? I was fed up by this time. I took the engagement ring off and threw it across the room. I can't remember if he apologized or not, but he walked across the room, picked up the ring and eventually returned it to the jewelry store.

We were in a downward spiral, but somehow, we still carried on like a couple. He went to church with me every Sunday, and we stopped for lunch before going home. I still went to work every day, and he still borrowed my car every now and then. Soon, he became more aggressive with his jealous accusations. He would periodically accuse me of seeing other men. When my granddaughter texted me—sending me her cute rockets that would sparkle on my phone and make me smile, he assumed they were messages from a man. I would always let him know that it wasn't a man, just my darling, Rachel, then just eleven or twelve years old, sending her grandmother sweet messages.

When he got a job at the airport cleaning airplanes on the night shift, he would call me while I was asleep, knowing I had to get up early for work. He called because he believed there was a man in my apartment. There was never any way to convince him otherwise. I was really getting tired of his behavior toward me. I was starting to pull back from him and he noticed.

One day, he had to go to the hospital and have some tests run on his heart. I went with him and was trying to reassure him that he was going to be fine. When the tests were completed, the doctor came in and said his heart was beating at maybe 50% or less, so we went home and he began to tell me that I was acting differently towards him, like I'd lost interest. I was just sick of his insecure behavior.

My birthday was coming up in July. I had made a big deal celebrating his birthday and it seemed like he was going to do the same for me. I noticed, though, as the day approached, he became antsy and fidgety. He took me to my favorite soul food restaurant, owned by Evander Holyfield. As I was eating, he was getting more antsy, and he would get up from the table and walk away and sometimes say something to the staff. Maybe he was planning a surprise for me, I thought. I waited, thinking there must be something big waiting for me at home. But there wasn't, and I was disappointed.

One Sunday, when I got up to go to church, he said he wasn't going. Well, that was sorta strange and it was the first time that had happened. So I went on to church and had a wonderful time. One of the older ladies in the Church came over to me and said she had a message for me that God wanted her to share. I listened and thanked her for her words. After service, I had lunch with one of my dear girlfriends, from whom I had rented some space in her home a few years prior while I worked at the Group Home. I would use the space I rented to get away on the weekends. We had a wonderful time catching up. We reminisced about the fun times, like going to the Jazz Clubs in Midtown to listen to live music and to sip on some wine and also, going shopping. I shared with her that I thought I was ready to move from my place.

She said, "What about your boyfriend?"

I said, "Oh, he can get an apartment of his own."

She immediately offered me my old bedroom and bathroom at the same rate as before, and I said, "Hmmm, that sounds like a good idea."

When it was time to go home, I figured I'd mention to my boyfriend that I was going to move. When I did, I suggested that we could still get married later, but I was going to move back with my friend to save some money.

He didn't say much. He just went to the store for a gallon of milk. When he came back home, he was acting uneasy again. Little did I know that all hell was about to break loose.

I was sitting in my living room in my recliner. He walked over to the front window and screwed the mini blinds shut. I am not sure what happened after that. I guess the shock and adrenaline took over. All I remember is that we were tussling. He was pushing and pulling and shoving me, and I was doing my best to protect myself. I was trying to get away from him. I went to my bedroom and he followed me there.

He then pulled out my ice pick that I had hidden for protection. He was trying to use it on me. Then he uttered those words that I had only heard on television, "If I can't have you, nobody else will."

He said, "I know you've got other men putting money in your account," which was lies, all lies. Then he threw me on my bed and pinned me down with his knees on each inner elbow. Now, he was straddled over me. He still had the ice pick in his hand and was going for my face. I quickly turned my head.

By that time, all I could think about were my four darling children. I could see their faces. I needed to live for them. Seeing their faces gave me enough strength to push him off of me. I tried to grab my land line and he grabbed that from me. I ran to the living room and started knocking and banging on the wall I shared with his nephew's apartment next door. I was screaming, "Help me! He's trying to kill me!"

The nephew's wife was home from work that Sunday, and heard me from her bedroom. She and the nephew came outside, approached my front door and tried to get in.

He had me struggling on the floor, as he was trying to run the ice pick through the back of my skull. I screamed, "Break the window! Take my flower stand and break the window!"

Every time I reached for the door to unlock it, he would twist it, locking it back. That happened several times. I yelled, "Call the police!" Thankfully, they did. The flower stand did not break the double paned windows, but somehow, I got off the floor and unlocked the door.

Maybe his health challenges gave me some advantage. His nephew got in and pulled him off of me. The police arrived, took him outside and put him on the ground in the drizzling rain. I was free.

I had willed myself to live for my children, who mean the world to me. Their dad and I divorced when they were young. I took my children with me to Baltimore after leaving their father, but there were times over the years when we were separated from each other when their father had custody. The years without them were almost unbearable at times and since then we've cherished each other and every moment together. This is why I had to will myself to live.

The policewoman asked to see the ice pick wounds. I showed her my chest, the side of my breast, and the back of my head, where he had only barely nicked the surface, thank God. I tried to get the blood off of the carpet in the living room, but I couldn't. And I also had to pay for the damage to the outside window. Needless to say, I didn't get all my security deposit back....But I got my life back. There was also a huge bruise on my left shoulder about three to four inches in diameter. But again, I'm still here by the grace of God.

And after all of that, I still had to go to work the next morning. My body was in spasms as I tried to walk and work. I cared for the son of a very wealthy man, and I couldn't call him and tell him what happened. He was not a lenient boss and I needed my job. Although the ice pick never penetrated my skull to do any real physical harm, there was plenty of mental and emotional damage.

I pressed charges.

I ended up having to go before the grand jury and no one could come with me. It was one of the hardest things to sit through alone. The next weekend, my baby girl flew in. She took me to get boxes and helped me pack for my move.

To fast forward, I got back on the track of

ministry. An opportunity opened up for Sunday School teachers at my church and my girlfriend said, "Why don't you apply?" I did and I got hired and I've not turned back since.

With God's Grace

Delois Butler

"Whatever your hands find to do, do it with all your might."

—Church motto

I am the first born of eleven siblings from a small country farm in Manila, Arkansas.

This is where I was born. My parents left the farm when I was nine years of age to move to El Paso, Texas. I graduated from high school and went to college for one and a half years in El Paso. While in college, I met my first boyfriend, Jimmy M. Butler, who was in the U.S. Army and was also a minister from Houston, Texas. After dating for about a year, we decided to get married and we set the date for July, 1971. By this time, I had stopped my college career and found a job. We stayed in El Paso for one year and one baby before we moved to my husband's hometown of Houston.

After we started our new life in Houston, my

husband told me he had been called by God to go into full time ministry. As his wife, I was a little concerned.

"Are you sure this was the Lord's voice?" I asked.

"Yes," he replied.

"Then I am here to stand with you," I pledged.

Well, we did start a church with a small membership. We experienced many trials, tests, and opposition, but my husband was a man with a vision for every step we took. And so, we experienced many triumphs, too.

As the wife of a pastor, I took on several roles—choir director, prayer leader, even helping clean the church. Oh my, I was busy. Not to forget, I was also a wife and the mother of four wonderful children, three boys and one girl. The church motto: *whatever your hands find to do, do it with all your might.* Yep, that's what I did.

After seventeen years of marriage, the tables turned in our lives. I remember my husband asking me to take him to the hospital for a checkup. I did not know all the details. I just remember he told me the doctor had given him about five bottles of the laxative, Senokot, to take because, as my husband stated, his "bowel was all the way up to his neck" when the doctor had gotten the results from his x-rays. I was very disturbed by this information, and still he did not tell me all the details of what really was going on with him. So my next thought was that I needed to pray, and that's what I did.

He went back into the VA hospital and the next thing I knew, the doctors stated that they would have to keep him. Oh my, what is going on with my husband? He was not able to come home for days, and then weeks. Each time I went to visit, I was speechless.

I was thirty-seven years old at that time. My husband was only thirty-nine.

I had many questions about what was going on that I never got answered. The doctor stated, "Your husband has walking pneumonia and we are trying to keep it from spreading throughout his lungs." My husband was a very active young man. He pastored our church with focus and energy. He appeared tireless, making himself available to the many obligations of the ministry. I knew something was not right when he could not get rid of a cough, but I couldn't imagine that this was so severe that it would lead to his death.

After about a week in the hospital, he got worse instead of better. I was just in shock. So were our children. It was difficult to even bring them to the hospital, and difficult for them to see their dad in this condition.

Our congregation prayed for his recovery, along with our family in El Paso. At the end of May, 1988, at 12 midnight, I received a call from the VA hospital to come immediately. One of our deacons met me there. When I arrived, the doctors told me I needed to sign papers to grant them permission to put my husband on life support. You just can't imagine how I felt, and the things going on in my head, even though I knew God was my only hope. I signed the paperwork and prayed for God to give my husband complete healing. The doctors had given him antibiotics and were doing everything they knew to help him get well.

They moved him to a room and only one person could visit at a time. Since I was his wife, I could visit more often. The time in that room with my husband fading away from me was like a nightmare, and my thoughts were, "This too will pass. God is not through with him yet." I was unprepared. All I could do was hold on to the hope of recovery, like a sinking raft in a raging river.

Each time I went in the room, I was speaking words of hope and healing. He started asking for water, and I thought this was a good sign. But the doctors said he could not have water. I asked why, but in my cloud of disappointment and despair, I just can't remember what was said to me. Then my husband called out all of our children's names, asking me where they were. I told him they were in school. And just before he closed his eyes, he mouthed the words, "I love you."

The machine went code blue. I was paralyzed, numb, speechless. I could not believe this was happening. I couldn't even cry. The hospital brought his body out before taking him to another room and I just laid on his chest, in silence.

I walked out of the hospital in a state I never imagined for myself. A single parent, with four children- ages seventeen, fifteen, thirteen, and twelve. It was a new beginning, but not a welcome one. We had no insurance, but thank God the COGIC denomination we were affiliated with helped us out tremendously. I must say, I was so thankful to everyone who was there for us. Friends, family and our church members showed up to support, feed and tend to our needs.

But then, after the funeral, the stream of calls and offers of food and assistance ceased and we were alone. You ask yourself, where are all the people that once knew us? Where are those that said they loved us? It was quiet, as if we were forgotten. I had to encourage myself and keep going. So thankful for my relationship with God, I began my new position as head of the house and I went back to work.

At work, I noticed as each day passed, my manager kept watching me without saying anything. The next thing I knew, he brought me in the office to tell me I was incompetent and he would have to let me go. I found myself jobless with social security as my only income. I prayed and asked God to tell me which direction I should take.

I decided to go back to college. In fact, I attended a business college to become a legal secretary. I passed the course, but could not find placement in that field. I was disappointed that attorneys wanted a more experienced person in the field and would not take a chance on a fresh and eager graduate. I ended up getting a job as a secretary with a transformer company. The job did not pay well but I did the work, trusting that God would supply our needs. And he did.

When this job ended, I remembered that I still had my cosmetology license. So I got a job at Supercuts as a haircutter. Working at Supercuts was fun and I really liked the job. I had built up a good clientele. After getting off of work, I would come home some nights and feel so alone, but deep down within I knew God was there. When I look back, I realize that God was teaching me to trust him no matter what, and to trust myself. In the midst of grief and the trauma of sudden loss, I had to really stay focused. Even though I made some wrong choices, I never had a desire to just give up. I had too much at stake.

I remember when my car kept getting hot and breaking down on the freeway. Oh my, I didn't know a mechanic. I didn't have anyone to call. Standing on the freeway shoulder, I was hoping someone, anyone, would stop and help. Nobody came to my aid. And yet, it was probably best that I didn't have any dangerous encounters. Thank God, I remembered that I had purchased AAA insurance. Yeah for being wise enough to have a back-up!

Our living environment that my husband had left us in was not a good location, and I knew this was not where God wanted us to stay. One of my sisters referred me to a realtor and God told me to ask him for the kind of house I wanted. So I did. The realtor asked me where I wanted to live, and we looked in that area. I found the house I wanted but I did not have the credit to buy it. Because everything was in my husband's name, the banks turned me down. Every time a loan officer said, "You should try another bank," I kept speaking that the house was mine, and wherever the sole of my feet tread, He would give it to me.

Finally, the realtor sent paperwork into HUD and I was approved for a loan. Hallelujah, we had our own house!

I had to encourage myself on every decision. Providing for my family was not always the easiest, but I believed nothing was impossible with God. My children also struggled after their father's passing. As a parent, I had to be on guard regarding the friends they chose or the friends that chose them, which brought about a lot of challenges and temptations. As a single parent with teenagers, I had to be very focused and prayerful. I had to realize my children were grieving over the absence of their father, as I was over the loss of my spouse.

While my children were in high school, each one of my sons got jobs at various fast-food restaurants, enabling them to help by buying their own clothes and food. I had told them from the very beginning that we were together in this. Thank God, everyone graduated from high school. I was so happy to see each of my children receive their high school diplomas. I could take a deep breath of relief that we made it through those high school years.

Right after high school, my second child decided to enlist in the Army, and I didn't know until the day he told me that he had his papers to leave. My other two sons took me down a journey of prison for a few years and that was a dark moment for me to go through. To see your child in a place you never thought in your wildest dreams you would ever visit. I made up in my mind that I would find my two sons wherever their locations and visit as much as I could. Each visit was so special to me. To be able to keep them informed of what was happening in the outside world. I wrote letters of encouragement to them even when I, myself, needed encouraging. But when you love your family, nothing is out of your way.

My only daughter, who is also the youngest, blessed me with three beautiful granddaughters. I had to realize that I could not make the desires that I had for my children cause me to be despondent about the choices they made for themselves. I had to learn (and am still learning) to get out of the way and let God do what he knew best.

So, while working at Supercuts, I asked God to bless me with a better job with good benefits. One day, while driving across town, a thought came across my mind to put an application in at the airport. So I followed the thought and at that time, Southwest Airlines was accepting applications in person. I submitted my application that very day. Then, one day, as I was walking out of the house to go to work at Supercuts, my house phone rang, and this beautiful voice on the line said,

"Hi, is this Delois?"

I said, "Yes."

"This is Southwest Airlines. Would you still be interested in the job you applied for?"

Well, my reply was, "Oh yes I would!"

I was so excited! When I got to Supercuts that day, I shared the news with my supervisor, who was happy for me and told me that I could keep my job at Supercuts through the probationary period with Southwest Airlines. That was a God moment again. Favor will surround you when you put your trust in Him. Now, with Southwest Airlines, thank God, I had a good job and we had a roof over our heads.

I say a roof over "our" heads because three of my

children came back to live with me several times. That was a lesson in itself.

As a parent, you question yourself, "Did I not teach or model a life that would propel them to adulthood?" There was no guidebook that gave me the road map for raising a family. I had to ask forgiveness sometimes. Sometimes, I had to ask God what was he teaching me in this? I had to realize that in life, I just had to walk through the journey and have faith that I would eventually see the good out of all of it.

At this time, I was still in the house God had given me after my husband passed. I completed my probation, started my new job and worked for Southwest Airlines for almost twelve years. It had been such a blessing for me and my family. We traveled to places I had only dreamt about as a child.

In time, I went to God again and told him I would like a house built from the ground up, where no one had lived before. I knew the word of God said that I could ask what I will and it shall be done unto me. My daughter and I started looking around in a neighborhood I really liked. I put my house up for sale, packed boxes as if I was already approved, and I believed I was by faith. I received so many distractions from people who wanted me to compromise what I had asked God for, just to discourage me. But I kept saying, "My house is sold. My house is sold," and I had a specific amount I wanted.

God said for me to write down what I wanted in the new house—bedrooms, bathrooms, flooring, etc., and not to deviate. So I did. Contractors started building the house while my other house was not sold yet. And it wasn't even sold by the time the new house was completed. The builders placed a "For Sale" sign on my new house. I went to the builders and told them they could not sell this house. It was mine. God gave it to me. So the builder promised not to show my house to anyone. A few weeks later, my other house sold for my exact asking price. God answers prayer! Finally, we walked into our brand-new house.

When I look over my life, I see where God has been with me and my family every step of the way. Even though their father was not there to see every event—their high school graduations, the birth of his grandchildren, and his children grow into adulthood—I am grateful for the little things he instilled in them while he was alive. At this present moment, all in my family are doing well, my oldest son has a great job. My second son is a minister in Oklahoma. My third son has a great job. And my daughter has her own business as a hairdresser. I have seven beautiful grandchildren. I am retired, after 25 years of service. Each one of us has accomplished so much in our lives that I am so thankful for God's mercy and love toward us. Without a doubt, our dreams are coming to pass because it has already been predestinated by God before we were even born to conquer and fulfill our purpose.

The Birthday Party

Julie Jones-Butler

"This was just the beginning.
So… can you love after betrayal?"

I guess you could say I'm a people person. When there is a party, I'm ready because I love to spend quality time with family and friends. Growing up, I was the only girl in a house full of boys. I have three brothers and always longed for a sister. Having none, I sought the company of other girls every opportunity I could get. I had girl cousins, but let me say, these relationships were tricky. As children, sometimes my cousins were nice, and sometimes, not so nice. At times, they were the next best thing to having sisters. Sometimes, they were my best friends. But other times, they were the worst kind of enemy, the perfect antagonists, the villain. In this story, they are the villain.

Because I was alone in my household of boys, I spent a lot of time by myself. When I wasn't playing with my dolls, I would read and draw just to keep myself busy. I did play with my neighborhood friends, but after dark I was on my own again. So I had to be creative.

All of this time alone allowed me to develop a vivid and colorful imagination, during which I would have conversations with imaginary people and would practice what I would say. But I longed for real interaction and play time with others. So, when my mom mentioned we were going to my cousin Janet's birthday party, I was thrilled. Little did I know I would be betrayed by the very ones whom I loved the most. This party was an early turning point and the beginning of a theme that would show up in my life going forward. It was the first time I asked myself, can you love after betrayal? But it would not be the last.

Perhaps one of the reasons I was so excited to attend this party was because, in my family, as children, my siblings and I didn't enjoy big birthday celebrations. Instead, usually on my birthday, Mom baked my favorite chocolate cake. She would put candles on it. You know those pastel-colored candles in yellows, blues and pinks. And the whole family would sing happy birthday...year after year and I loved it. But this was not the same as having a big party with other children, a mound of gifts, party games and colorful favors. So, Mom announced the upcoming party on Saturday, and boy, my eyes lit up with excitement. I had to wait a whole week. At the age of ten, seven days leading up to a birthday party felt like an eternity. To fill the time, I started imagining what the party would be like.

I was beyond excited about getting together with other girls, so I envisioned myself laughing, talking, playing games and relating to them as friends and equals. I started preparing myself by planning what I would wear. Although I didn't have much, I appreciated what I had. I loved to dress nicely and look cute. So, I decided that I would wear my ruffled plaid short set. It was blue, lavender, yellow and white. And I would wear my clear jelly sandals. I thought this would be the perfect girly outfit for the party. I loved colors because they made me feel happy and energetic, just like a kid in the candy store.

I was confident that with the right outfit and my eager but easy-going personality, I would be the life of the party. It's strange how young people equate looking nice with being accepted. After all, I was only 10 years old at the time, and I thought appearance was everything. Now, my hair was going to be a challenge because my mom didn't comb hair very well. Most of the girls who were attending the party had long hair. So, immediately, I started worrying about my plats. My plats were going to be flying because my hair wasn't long enough. I never understood why my hair wouldn't lay down. It had a mind of its own. I hated when one plat would lie down and the other wouldn't. How do you tame beautiful kinky hair? At the time, I didn't think it was so beautiful.

Every day leading up to Saturday, I tried to imagine what would happen at the party—who would be there; what games would we play; how would I best communicate? I told my friend at school that I was going to a party on Saturday and I was excited. I know she could tell I didn't have birthday parties of my own, but now that I think about it, that probably didn't matter to her at all. But who knows? Maybe it did.

I cleaned my room every day just to pass time. I was moving things around to give the room a different look, which also made me happy. Before I knew it, Friday was here and the next day was the party. I went to bed early just to get to Saturday faster.

I woke up with pure excitement on Saturday morning and was eager to complete my chores. After cleaning, I watched *Fat Albert* and danced while watching *Soul Train*. Let me mention, I could cut a rug. Then, Mom said, let's comb your hair so we can be on time. Oh, boy...I knew that wasn't going to turn out well. But Mom and I did a good job. I was getting older, so I started trying to comb my own hair. This time, I helped get it right. We put stretchy bow knockers and white barrettes in my hair and my plats were lying perfectly. I put on my short set and jelly sandals and I was ready to go.

It was sunny, humid and hot, but not unbearable

for the South. I was accustomed to the Louisiana heat and I knew to prepare for those aggressive mosquitoes. Before leaving, I grabbed that orange can of Off bug spray.

When Mom said, "Let's go," I jumped into the passenger side of our blue Maverick and we headed to the party. I was smiling and talking while she was flying down the streets. She thought our Maverick was the best and fastest car, and always reminded me that this car could go. So, she put the pedal to the metal. And in a short time, we had arrived.

There were colorful balloons, a homemade cake, hot dogs, chips, tuna sandwiches, Shasta soda and lime sherbet punch. Everything was pretty, and the freshly baked cake made the kitchen smell like a bakery. Not only were there decorations inside the house but there were festive balloons and tables on the patio. I walked out the doors to where the children were gathered in the backyard and said hello. All the girls were talking and playing and I fit right in. My two cousins were among the group of girls. Janet, the birthday girl, and Belinda smiled and welcomed me into the group. I was happy to see that they had decided to be friend-cousins on this special day.

We played *Red Light, Green Light* in the middle of the freshly cut lawn. There were no mosquitoes and we were running, laughing and playing. We were just acting like little silly girls. We played hopscotch on the patio and I helped draw the squares with yellow chalk. Hopscotch was one of my favorite games and I was good at it. Thinking back, I recall everyone enjoying themselves. The party was as wonderful as I had imagined it would be right up to the moment cousin Janet said, "Let's have a balloon fight."

In my mind, I wondered why anyone would want to involve water balloons when we were all dressed so nicely and with hair combed so pretty. There was a pile of balloons on the table and we filled them all with water.

This is when one of my happiest moments turned into a nightmare. This is when my friend-cousins turned into villains. Janet and Belinda started throwing balloons at me and me only. Even now, I do not know why my cousins turned on me. I never understood what caused them to decide that they were going to be my enemies instead of my friends, when they were going to trade in our kinship bond for cruelty. But they often opted for cruelty, and that day was no exception. They pummeled me with water balloons, aiming for my face, until I was soaked from head to toe. My feet were sliding in my sandals. It happened so fast, I didn't even have time to say stop. I was standing there looking like a wet puppy and I knew that I looked a mess. My plats were no longer twisted, but were heavy with water and straight. My barrette was hanging off the end of my plat. When your permed hair gets wet, you not only look like a wet puppy, but a scarecrow, too. One girl said, "Stop hitting her like that," but they kept throwing, laughing and making fun of me. No one else was being hit the way I was. At least, that's what I remember. I felt embarrassed, defeated and helpless.

In my mind, I started thinking no one here likes me. That was when I started asking myself, was I too skinny, was my hair not combed right, and was I too dark because I was the darkest child at the party. My emotions were all over the place. Finally, it was time to eat and I was the only one at the table who was dripping wet. No adult cared to ask me why I was so wet. I don't think my mom noticed because she was talking with some of the other ladies.

I had built myself up with excitement and anticipation and was having fun. Now, I was crushed, let down, feeling isolated and different. It felt like someone had squeezed the life out of me. I don't know how I still managed to sing happy birthday to Janet, but I did. I smiled when I didn't want to. I tried to act as if it didn't bother me because I didn't want to bring any more attention to myself. But I wanted out and was ready to go home and get in my bed. I had to wait until the party ended. When we got in the car and headed home, it seemed like the Maverick had lost its speed.

Mom asked me if I had a good time, and I said, no. I told her what happened and she said they were kids and they were just playing. But I could feel in my spirit that there was more to it than just playing. I'm sure my cousins felt empowered when they ripped away my confidence. I told my mother that they enjoyed humiliating me in front of others when all I wanted to do was have a good time. I started looking out the window, holding back the tears. Finally, we made it home, thank God! I got out of the car, went in the house, took my bath and brushed my hair. Before climbing into bed, I said my prayers. I started reliving the events of the day. I didn't deserve that kind of treatment. I was a kind and friendly child. Then, again, I started questioning and blaming myself. Why did I think I could have fun at someone else's party? Was I being selfish? I just wanted everything to be perfect. My tears started flowing like a river. I pulled the covers over my head and I didn't want to ever feel like that again.

But I would. What I didn't realize then was this wouldn't be the last time my hopes would be pummeled by someone I thought I could trust. This was just the beginning. So, can you love after betrayal? It takes time and patience to heal. It's a journey that makes you stronger each time you are betrayed. But I wasn't there yet. After all, I was a child just wanting to belong.

Altar Call

Koinonia I. Martin-Page

"Speak to me! God is trying to tell you something!"

—Shug Avery, *The Color Purple*

In the Fall of 2020, I found my forty-plus-year-old-self re-enrolled in grade school. No, I had not been cast in another remake of the movie *Big*. Like countless other parents at the beginning of the pandemic, I was quarantined at home with my family, and my children were enrolled in a remote virtual school program. At times, I couldn't tell whether remote school was a blessing or a curse. On the one hand, it was a blessing to have this COVID-safe option for my three kids and to have that option provide insight into what was happening in their classrooms. On the other hand, it was an option that gave me insight into what was happening in their classrooms. Shining a light in a dark space is not always blessed work. It can feel like disturbing a sleepy log in the woods. You roll it over to the sunlight, and all manner of bugs—some cute and some nightmarish—come out. With the kids attending school online at home, I was able to see what was crawling and festering underneath the log. I was among the congregation of families with Black kids in school, in the wake of the murder of George Floyd, and in the midst of a pandemic. I was in the front pew witnessing the challenging classroom experiences Black grade school students can have.

Other parents in this congregation probably know these experiences all too well. Even so, it can still be painful and exhausting. How many times should one Black child endure having his technical difficulties or his confusion about an assignment mislabeled as "misbehavior"? How do you help a White teacher empathize and see that your Black boy's urgent need to go to the bathroom is not him being "unruly" or "defiant"? How do you help a White teacher discern that Black boys can be playful and "rambunctious," too, and it doesn't mean they should be regarded as nascent criminals? How many times do you have to patiently explain to teachers that the "immigration" assignment, which asks your child, a descendant of enslaved Black people, to discuss the decision of his ancestors to immigrate to the United States, is racially biased or in the least, does not feel designed with Black, Native, or undocumented students in mind? How often do you need to meet with a teacher, and how many emails do you need to write, to get her to understand that you expect the same attention and feedback as the White mothers receive about your child's progress?

One morning, I went into my bathroom, feeling particularly overwhelmed and depleted. I needed to conjure up a tent revival. I'd come to my bathroom mirror altar to lament, to reflect, to reckon, and to lay my burdens down. I'd come to pray for answers with the minister-preacher-healer reflected in the mirror. More creepy-crawly bugs had come to light in my babies' classes.

I am a veteran advocate for my Black boys in education. When my oldest was just five, he came home and told me how the dark-skinned kids had been separated from the light-skinned kids in his class. So, I had to have a come-to-Jesus meeting with his teacher and the school director. It has felt like every year, for each of my children, new issues pop up like whack-a-mole. I came to learn that I couldn't Montessori school them away, private school them away, or highly ranked public school them away. These issues existed whether rich or poor, and even persisted in the face of my sons' pristine report cards and test scores. (Don't play with this Black mama. Them grades better be on point!) These issues had sprung up again, now with my fourteen, eleven, and nine-year-olds in school, online. What was advocacy for them supposed to look like now? There I was in my bathroom "prayer closet," alternating between balled-up-fist-Sophia-from-The-Color Purple-mad, and bathrobe-clenched-Oh-Mary-Don'tcha-Weep-worried. I was tarrying for answers to help my Black sons. I was tired. I surrendered. Then, I began to remember.

A couple of decades earlier, before I was in *that* bathroom, I had been in another bathroom, looking for answers in the mirror. I was cold and a little scared. My French roll with the front swoop hairstyle was still fresh from senior prom. It had been a warm and sunny April day when I'd left Florida for Connecticut a couple days beforehand. When I made it to Yale's campus in New Haven, though, that cold slapped me so hard in the face, I thought maybe I'd said something bad about her mama. How could it be so ungodly cold in April? On top of that, I had been walking around buildings anxiously expecting the Joker to jump out at me at any moment. Pointed arches, vaults, flying buttresses, gargoyles, and stained-glass windows. It was straight outta Batman. Gotham City was the only other place where I'd seen so much Gothic architecture. I had been housed for the weekend with a sophomore named Dorcas. A late '90s version of Alexandria Ocasio Cortez, Dorcas must have been a member of each and every student leadership group on campus. She took me 'round to all her meetings, including the Black Student Union, or "BSAY" (for Black Student

Alliance at Yale), and a group that called itself "COFAR" for Coalition for Financial Aid Reform.

At the COFAR meeting, even though I was just a visiting pre-frosh, the student leaders there encouraged me to share my experience with the financial aid process. I could almost hear my mama's voice in my head, "Don't you tell my business!" but something told me to take a risk. So I shared the sad experience I'd had at the financial aid office earlier that day. I recounted how the financial aid counselor had slammed the empty financial aid folder in my face. (She really didn't slam it, but boy, that's what it felt like to my pitiful self!) She grimly explained that my folder was empty because I had been granted zero financial assistance. I had failed to submit my noncustodial parent information. Without it, the financial aid counselors couldn't prepare a financial aid package for me.

At hearing this from her, I left my body. I was supposed to be on my way as a first-generation college student and the first Black person from my tri-county area to go to an Ivy League school. My mom had sacrificed for this. My grandma and 'nem, my sweet granddaddy, with just a third-grade education, were all counting on me. Yet, I was from a single-parent home of low-to-no economic means, so no financial aid package most assuredly meant that I would not be matriculating at Yale. At that time, it was Yale policy to require financial information from both parents. This policy was based on the well-intended principle that both parents should be responsible for their child's tuition costs. I couldn't believe it. Even if I *could* have submitted the noncustodial parent information, my father was not going to be contributing a doggone thing to my college tuition anyway. It still would be my mother and me who would bear the financial burden. So, while well-meaning, the policy unintentionally shut students like me out of receiving a financial aid package at all.

I knew my noncustodial parent was alive and living somewhere in my hometown, but at the time, I couldn't have told you where that was or anything about his financial circumstances. A Vietnam War vet, he'd suffered from post-traumatic stress disorder, and because of it, he developed a severe drug and alcohol addiction. When he did live with us, he brutally terrorized me, my mom, and my three siblings. At several points in time, we'd had to hide from him. He'd done things like chase my cancer-stricken, underwear-clad, older brother out of the house at gunpoint. He'd kidnapped me at gunpoint from my grandparents' house when I was seven years old only to bring me back because he was disgusted by how terrified I was of him. He would brutally beat my mother mercilessly in front of us four kids, without caring that all the neighborhood could hear, too. His drug habit put us in such dire financial straits that we often had utilities disconnected and eventually, we lost our home to foreclosure. After every night of terror, I would still have to go to school and deliver a gold medal academic performance, as if I were in the Academic Olympics, because my mama didn't play that. Them grades better be on point! And I couldn't tell a living soul about the war zone going on at home. So, even though I'd worked my butt off, and overcome impossible odds to be admitted to Yale, it felt like my dad's craziness, combined with Yale's policy, meant that my dream had ended there, in an empty financial aid folder.

After hearing my story, the COFAR president asked me to share it the next morning at a protest meeting with Yale administrators. My story highlighted COFAR's mission to protest and change the unfair financial policies at Yale and other Ivy League schools. These financial aid policies disproportionately disadvantaged students of color, which most of the COFAR students looked to be. These policies meant that even after overcoming historical barriers to earn a place in the student body, those students would be saddled with oppressive debt once they graduated, unlike their more affluent classmates. Although the COFAR leaders could've shared my story at the meeting themselves, they couldn't tell it like I could. They believed that it might have more of an impact if I showed up and shared my experience myself. Now, I had already defied my mama's "don't-tell-my-business" rule once, but now these COFAR agitators were asking me to embarrass my mama again tomorrow in front of what would presumably be a whole bunch of white folks in the Yale administration! Lord-help-me, I had to go to the bathroom!

And so there I was, cold, scared, looking in the mirror, and praying for an answer. Somehow in that bathroom mirror, *my soul said yes,* because the next morning, I found myself seated at the table with the Yale financial aid director, the Yale College dean, several other administrators, and the COFAR student leaders. I awaited my turn to share my story, and share I did. As my dear friend would say, I did a "reveal-to-heal." I did not hold back. Cornbread-fed and southern-fried, I testified! No one else at that table had my story. They hadn't envisioned me, or others like me, when they were making and implementing this financial aid policy. When I came to the table and spoke, I exposed to the policy makers what they hadn't been able to see. In telling my story, I advocated for myself and other students like me.

That advocacy changed the trajectory of my life. The administrators reversed the financial aid determination that had left my financial aid folder empty, and I went on to receive a financial aid package and matriculate at Yale. In a small way, that advocacy also furthered the efforts of student protesters, like the ones in COFAR, and each year since, the financial aid policies for first-generation, low-income students have continued to improve. Today, financial aid policies and packages for first-generation, low-income students at Yale look so much better than they did in the late nineties. Hallelujah!

As I remembered those lessons from my own story, I could see what advocacy for my children needed to look like. Of course, I would always be there to speak up for them, but I also needed to empower them to advocate for themselves. They are stakeholders in their own academic journeys, and they should be respected and engaged in that manner. They needed to be at the table to speak for themselves because no one can tell their stories and experiences like they can. Their authentic stories, in *their* voices, are powerful to reveal, heal, transform, summon support, and effect change. That powerful potential is there, even if there's some anxiety, too, along the way.

My four-decade-year-old-self came back into focus in the mirror. I could almost hear Shug Avery singing, *"Speak to me! God's trying to tell you something!"* I looked gratefully into the eyes of the minister, then raised my hands in thanks. With hope rising in my heart, I left the altar revived, renewed, and ready.

Through the Eyes of the Little Girl

Cyntara Sanders

"I became my own savior."

Up early in the morning to see my mommy off to work. She would leave while it was still dark outside. My dad would walk her to the bus stop and then care for my baby sister and me for the rest of the day. I recall so vividly this day, walking into my bedroom, looking up at my dad while he was changing my sister's diaper. My sister and I are five years apart, so I was around five years old.

"Daddy, I'm hungry, can I have an egg and cheese sandwich?" I asked.

It was still very early in the morning, so he told me he would fix it in a little while. After watching cartoons for some time, I went to look out of the living room window at the swimming pool. I liked to stare at the pool that was in the middle of our apartment complex. We lived in a downstairs apartment unit directly in front of the pool. I loved going swimming or just being near pools or beaches. I enjoyed the sounds of the water splashing, people talking, and children laughing and playing. Even though I couldn't swim, I loved getting in the pool.

"Daddy, I'm still hungry, can I have the sandwich now and go swimming later?" I asked. He told me I would have to do something special for him before I could eat and go swimming, something to make him feel good first. As I followed him into the bathroom, I knew then what was about to happen. It wasn't the first time. But this is the memory that constantly presents itself even these many years later. He sat on the edge of the tub, unzipped his pants and asked me to open my mouth. Then I went to a place in my mind where I would often escape, a black hole where I could just get away and sit. I was despondent and in a world of my own. Later, though, I escaped into the cartoon shows, ate my sandwich and happily waited for the pool to open. I was the first one in, excited and happy to play in the pool for as long as possible.

TRAUMA

We moved to another apartment. As I was playing in this bedroom, which was on the other side of the hallway with only a bathroom between Mommy and Daddy's room and mine, I heard a noise and went running into my parents' room. My mom was lying with her head in my dad's hand, and her body, lying across the bed, was limp and lifeless. Her eyes were closed. I stared from their door. "What's wrong with Mommy?" I asked.

Instead of answering my question, Daddy asked me to get a cold towel. I was paralyzed with fear, unable to move. He had to repeat himself, "Cyntara, get me a cold towel."

I finally snapped out of it, got the cold towel and handed it to him. I watched as he laid the wet, cold towel on my mommy's face, gently patting her face with it. She began waking up. I took in a deep breath, relieved. In a soft, faint voice she asked, "What happened?"

My dad said my mommy was just fine and told me to leave the room.

TRAUMA

I was playing in my room, which was facing east of the living room on the other side of the apartment. The scenery is different in my memory, so we must have moved again. My parent's door was open and I could hear them arguing. As I stood there listening to see what the commotion was about, the door suddenly slammed shut. A decorative candle holder that was nailed to the top of the door fell on my nose. I began screaming and crying from the pain. They both came out to look after me. This accident caused them to stop fighting. From that moment, I realized the power that harm to myself could wield in the name of keeping the peace. This was, I learned, what martyrdom looked like. I still have the scar on my nose.

TRAUMA

Some years had passed and my mommy and dad were no longer together. Now, it was just my mom, my baby sister and me. Mom would sometimes work two jobs to care for us. She didn't have a car and we were receiving food stamps to purchase food. Often, we would catch the Metro bus with her. I enjoyed riding the bus. It felt like an adventure. Sometimes, when we could not go with her, my mom would call Popsqually to babysit my sister and me. Popsqually was an old man who lived in the same small six or seven-unit apartment building as we did. Sometimes, I would have to go to his house to wait on the school bus because my mom would have to catch the bus for work very early in the morning. There would also be times when we might have to go to his house after school. Popsqually was wheelchair-bound due to having both legs amputated.

He was cooking the day I came over after school in my seventh year—some hot water cornbread, chicken and greens. He was a pretty good cook and I enjoyed eating his food. As I was coming out of the restroom, he called me into his bedroom. He had a small, dark cup that he was using and I could hear a strange suctioning noise.

"Come in. I want you to use this cup on me," he said, demonstrating an up and down stroke with the awkward-looking cup near his privates. I was so scared and frustrated.

Why are you asking a seven-year-old to do these strange things? I'm just a kid! I argued in my mind. But the only words that came out were, "I don't want to," and I left the room. I sat in the living room watching Sesame Street, dazed and uneasy. Not too long after I ate, it was time to go home.

TRAUMA

My mom had small house parties from time-to-time on the weekends with a few friends and family. She had such a great vinyl collection. She would play Rick James, Michael Jackson, Sheila E, Tina Turner, Prince and so many more R&B greats and different genres. My uncle Rodger would come over from time-to-time and when he saw me, he would always kiss me on the mouth. I did not like him and I didn't know why. My mom's favorite drinks were daiquiri's and pina coladas. I enjoyed sneaking into her adult time to jam to the music and dance a bit.

But before long, I would get kicked out. Every now and again, they would smoke weed. One time, I snuck in on the fun and got a contact high. I danced in such a way that I had everyone laughing and enjoying my entertainment.

We were living in these same small unit apartments when Hurricane Alicia hit. I was still seven years old and I didn't have a clue about the devastation surrounding us. After the hurricane passed through, leaving such intense flood waters and so much destruction, I remember coming outside, playing in the water and walking around with my mom as she checked on the neighbors that we knew. The house across the street seemed to take the worst beating. I'll never forget that day. Our electricity had gone out and we had to light candles. Somehow, I made the best time out of playing in the water and living by candlelight.

TRAUMA

We moved again, and by middle-school age, we were living in the Alief area of Houston, Texas. I went to Sharpstown Middle School when I was in the 6th grade. I had so much fun in school, which is one of the main reasons I enjoyed going to school so much. I knew so many people and was always playing jacks, hula hoop, hopscotch, or just running around being a silly kid.

My favorite teacher was Ms. Brown. She was transgender. Everyone talked about her being a man and would make fun of her. I couldn't stand to hear people talk about her in a negative way because she was always very nice, patient, and considerate of me. During class, there was this one little, scrawny white boy who would always run his mouth. This particular day, he wouldn't shut up after Ms. Brown corrected him more than twice. Something just came over me. I could no longer stand his blatant disrespect of my favorite teacher. I jumped out of my seat with lightning speed, slapped and punched him in rapid succession, and then calmly sat back down as if nothing had happened. Though it took a little while for the class' laughter to calm down, we were able to get through our lesson without any more of his disruptions. Ms. Brown didn't send me to the office, and I didn't get in trouble. She only smiled and said, "Well, you sure know how to shut someone up."

After class, the boy was ready for round two. He approached me to fight, but I turned him down and said, "You had your shot. I'm not getting in trouble. Get out of my way."

The older I got, the more I found myself in some type of fight, mostly those that I didn't start.

We moved a little bit farther down the street to the intersection of Spice and Cinnamon Lanes. Not too long after moving there, I joined this popular gang. From the outside looking in, the gang looked like a close-knit family that had fun. The gang members were always together in groups, enjoying each other's company. From the inside, it turned out, gang life wasn't fun whatsoever. Several members were stealing, robbing, breaking into homes, and even raping the women in the gang. I was one of the ones that got raped by a guy name Slim. For a time, I was the female version of Slim. I used to sneak out of my bedroom window from time to time searching for excitement or some type of fun. One night, I let him sneak into my bedroom through the window. It was the worst mistake ever. He told me if I didn't have sex with him, he would make a lot of noise and wake up my mom. I got out of that gang by disassociating myself from them. So many members were getting killed or put in jail. I wanted no part of what they stood for. The fun and family bonding I sought was a promise unkept.

TRAUMA

There was a young girl who was brown-skinned and slim like me who I instantly connected with in my apartments. We would walk to school together or catch the bus. Her name was Tisha. She was one of my best friends. After school, she and I would be at each other's house after completing our homework. Sometimes, I did her hair, and other times, she did mine. We loved to wear those pony tails you add on after you spritz with hairspray, apply rollers, then put in the microwave to curl faster. If we were not at one another's home, we talked on the phone for hours. When Tisha came over to my house on this particular day, I was washing dishes. My phone rang, so I asked her to answer it for me.

"Hello?" she said into the phone. There was a pause and then her mouth fell open with a shocked expression. She quickly hung up.

"Girl, I don't know who that man is, but he said he's on his way to fuck the shit out of you."

I was terrified and didn't know what to do. I asked her not to leave. I looked at the caller ID and saw that, sure enough, it was my Uncle Rodger, the one I'd hated for my entire childhood. He had never touched me other than to kiss my lips in front of all the adults whenever he was in my presence. I called my mother, who sounded more frustrated with me than concerned after I told her exactly what happened. Not too long after speaking with my mom, Uncle Rodger's wife called and apologized. She later found out he had been sexually abusing their deaf and mentally challenged daughter.

TRAUMA

These are not the sum total of my trauma as a little girl, only a window into my memory.

Unfortunately, it doesn't stop here. My brother's father, knowing about my past traumas, assaulted me twice. In previous years, while I was in middle school, he and my mom took me to speak with a counselor when I finally shared what my dad had done to me. I thought I could trust him. And last but certainly not least, my pastor sexually assaulted me for years. This man of God had officiated my marriage. I had received "counseling" from him to help me get through my previous traumas. I thought I was safe in his care and believed he was my savior, a father figure and spiritual guide wrapped up in one person. But the entire time we were together, I was being groomed. Before I knew it, I was a twenty-something little girl without a voice and not a soul around to help me. I spent over ten years going to his church, serving in ministry, working for the church as a full-time employee at one point and working for him in his outside business. I had become so isolated. My routine was going to work, then home, then church—work, home, church. I became so depressed and at one point, suicidal.

One day, I was watching *The Oprah Show* when she had a panel of men who confessed their abuse of children, including their own. As I watched the show, I had so many light bulb moments and finally had language for all of the emotional, physical and psychological abuse I had suffered throughout my childhood and young adult life. The program gave me the whys and hows behind what had happened to me. I felt that I was armed with so much wisdom and I felt so empowered after watching just that one episode. Because of the grooming by all of my abusers, I had so much mistrust in myself, so much rage, insecurity, self- hatred, doubt and fear. I was so accustomed to my own destructive, harsh self-talk and self-sabotaging ways.

I finally realized after starting my healing journey, which swiftly began seven years ago after that Aha moment, that my isolation was part of the package. I finally built up the courage to tell my husband what the pastor had been doing to me. He couldn't accept what I told him. He wanted a divorce and left me a week later. I, by this time, was the mother of two middle-school-aged children. Now, I was alone, extremely depressed, suicidal and hearing voices that told me to kill myself.

Mutual friends informed me that my husband was telling people that I had an affair with the pastor, instead of telling the truth. During this time, I went through the most excruciating pain that I don't wish on anyone. Looking back, I call it my dark night of the soul. I felt I had no choice but to address all of my issues. I tried counseling, then a spiritual therapist. I began going deeper within myself, speaking daily affirmations while facing my reflection in the mirror, praying and talking to my spirit guides, ancestors and angels. I had some energy healing work done on me and then began taking classes and reading more about all types of healing modalities. For me, it turned out that the best medicine was to remove all the band-aids at once. I realized that there was no one who would heal me. I became my own savior.

As I continue this journey, I have daily rituals that bring me peace, love and wellness. Some of the things that have helped me to become an overcomer of these traumas are daily breath work, meditations, affirmations, kemetic yoga, nature walks, self-Reiki, as well as growing and eating magic mushrooms. I've benefited from classes in shadow work, childhood healing and sitting in my power, and I've subscribed to all things that affirm who I am and why I am on this Earth. I now enjoy guiding others to do the same. I understand now why I reincarnated into this world with so much trauma. I am here to assist those who desire healing, guidance and strength, and to show others the healer within.

Three Days, Three Months, Thirty Years

Demitri Sargent

"We all eat lies when our hearts are hungry."

It was exactly one month and a day before my twenty-second birthday. I was green as grass, as my daddy would say. Daddy was a Baptist preacher, and really all I knew was church and church people. My parents divorced when I was in the sixth grade. One might say, I was rather sheltered and inexperienced with the male species. I dated like any girl my age, going out for an occasional movie or dinner but nothing all that serious.

A family friend with whom I attended church, spent a lot of time at our house. My mother was always inviting somebody to dine with us for Sunday dinners after church. She'd make things like pot roast, fresh snapped string beans with potatoes, hand shucked corn on the cob, pickled beets, tossed salad, hot buttered rolls and sweet tea. Oh and dessert, there was always dessert—pound cake, banana pudding, sock-it-to-me cake...all made with love. The notorious church nap would soon follow after one of her Southern Sunday meals.

Richard was one of the young ministers on staff at the church. Tall, skinny, awkward, goofy, with a good sense of humor. He was very committed to ministry and wasn't very close to his family. Mama took a liking to him, so she'd invite him over most Sundays so he could be with something like a family. He'd gotten wind of a guy who would visit our church from time to time who'd expressed interest in meeting me. I was seeing someone at the time, but Richard went on and on about how the guy was the pastor's nephew and was also a minister, and how nice of a guy he was. So I agreed to meet him.

As a young girl, I'd vowed never to date, let alone marry, a preacher because I understood they were to be strictly committed to the church and God's people. I saw that my father's Baptist conventions, meetings and even seminary were a priority that always seemed to come before our family. We never took family vacations. So men of God only had time for God, in my mind. No thanks, I secretly thought. I envisioned my husband taking me on elaborate vacations, and seeing the world with my children. Boy, did I dream that one up!

Richard asked me if I could go with him to visit

a friend of his in the hospital. His friend was the guy he'd mentioned who was interested in meeting me. Even in a hospital bed, I could see that he was the charismatic, energetic, smooth-talking, all-eyes-on-me type. He told us this wild story about how all the stress he was going through had landed him in the hospital. Richard introduced us, and his friend looked at me as if he could see through to my soul. I didn't feel in any way threatened because he was my pastor's nephew. But I certainly didn't expect what came next. With all the charm one could muster in a hospital gown, he said, "Hi, I'm Greg," as he reached to shake my hand. "Sorry to be finally meeting you under such drab conditions, but I think you should know you're going to be my wife."

I instinctively blurted out, "Nigga you must be crazy!" Then feeling self-conscious, I followed by replying, "With all due respect, you don't even know me." I was both shocked and intrigued by his candor. I didn't know whether to be offended or flattered. I gave him my number when he asked for it.

When Richard and I ended our visit and headed to the car, I inquired, "Did he bump his head?" Richard laughed as if my question wasn't valid. Greg's audacity had me quite curious. I couldn't tell if he was cocky or just confident. In my opinion, if you are just cocky, you are an attention whore. Cockiness screams insecurity. Still, I was shamelessly infatuated with the fact that a guy wanted to spend so much of his time with me. He even referred to me a few times as his soul mate.

Over the next few days, time seemed to fly as I was enraptured by the whirlwind of romance that kept me daydreaming and smiling into space—the long phone calls, beautiful, lush bouquets of flowers, fine chocolates, fancy gifts delivered in Neiman Marcus bags and boxes, and sexy candle lit dinner dates where I couldn't even eat my food. I was behaving like a lovesick schoolgirl. The constant flow of excessive attention was delightfully dizzying.

Steak and Ale was Greg's favorite restaurant. I didn't have a favorite anything just yet, so whatever he liked, I liked. I had very little experience with independence at this point. All of the excitement and never-ending compliments were new to me. So in all honesty, it felt like love.

Always dapper, donning the latest Brooks Brothers men's fashions, he knew how to make an entrance, his magical cologne announcing his presence before he appeared. Just the thought of his car pulling up made my heart skip a beat. I could hardly wait for his phone calls. It was as if I were under some sort of spell.

Early one morning, before work, he showed up at my house unannounced. I had no clue this was improper but my mother sure did.

"YES?" she scoffed, barely opening the door.

"Young man, do you know what time it is?" she said, her voice dripping with disdain.

"Hello, Ms. McDade. I know it's early, I just wa..."

I rushed to the door to see what merited this impromptu visit. I was equally anxious to save Greg from my mother's wrath. I could hear her about to blow as I moved between her and the barely opened door, loosening her mama-bear grip.

"I've got it from here, Mama," I said.

"He's gonna be real worrisome, you watch. He's up to something," she said in her most cavalier tone, intending for him to hear her prediction. I wanted to disappear. "Why is she being like this?" I pondered to myself.

There we were staring at each other through the thick awkward tension my mother left behind. Her comment sucked all the oxygen from the space, and now, it was hard to breathe. The somber mood was thwarted by the fragrant, colorful bouquet of flowers he was holding. All was immediately forgiven when our eyes met. With seamless finesse, he diminished my mother's insight in that moment. I was falling further into the abyss with each passing moment.

By day three, he was on one knee with a marriage proposal. I didn't have time to catch my breath. I barely had time to process who he really was—a twenty-three-year-old man, who was going through a divorce with baby number two on the way.

He'd conveyed every detail and indiscretion of his life that might remotely portray him in a less than stellar light in such a way that I'd see him as a victim of circumstance. This set up a defense in me should I hear any rumors against his character.

But I was in love. Not even my mama's insinuation that I was just marrying "the first thing to come along" could penetrate my psyche. Having been twenty-two herself at some point, I'm sure Mama deemed it futile to even attempt talking me out of our plans. Greg's gift of persuasion had me sold. He was a masterful storyteller. Aren't all preachers? Don't they all tell stories in such a way that moves you to feel like you can fly?

After announcing our very short engagement (only three months, to be exact), I recall the shocked response as most of our family and friends hadn't realized we were dating. Most of Greg's family were totally against the idea, and at times, he seemed unfazed by their lack of support. Privately, though, he'd expressed to me, in tears, how alone he felt about their disposition. Of course, I believed I was, all of a sudden, all he had in the world. In my mind, choosing me caused their alienation. My sense of obligation grew even deeper. Any obstacles to discourage us became fuel, as I made it my personal mission to prove everyone wrong. This is how things started off, anyway.

Exactly three months after our courthouse

marriage, we had a small, modest church wedding, no honeymoon. The next 30 years would prove to be the greatest lessons of my life.

There was love and happiness between us, but I rarely felt the sense of stability and rootedness that I craved. By year six, and the arrival of our second child, we had already moved five times. The impermanence started to bother me, and I began to feel emotionally disconnected around year fifteen. We'd had intense conversations about the elephant in the room, but we never came to a resolution.

What happened next is what occurs when life's little inconsistencies go unchecked.

I started to avoid the hard conversations about all the things married couples hate to talk about. My happiness was never a topic for discussion, so I started going within instead of sharing my feelings with my spouse. When I tried to open up about my feelings in the past, things always seemed to go intensely south, so I learned to keep my emotions to myself.

By now, we'd lived in too many places to count. We were living in our third hotel at this time. I'd grown concerned that my sons would be negatively affected by all of this uncertainty. I started to feel like my voice wasn't being heard as I tried to bring these concerns up to my husband. We would end up in an all-out war over simple things, usually related to money. I couldn't question a bill without a blow up.

The beginning of the end occurred one Friday night. I was working the second shift in a call center for an airline. I abhorred that job, especially working the second shift. The stress on the employees was so bad that on occasion co-workers would be taken to the hospital by ambulance due to anxiety. There was even a death. So I was both living and working in toxic environments. Mentally, I was in transition mode, and I made every attempt to remain focused on our goal to position ourselves and gain some stability.

This particular night, as I called to check on my husband's ETA to pick me up from work, the call went straight to voicemail. Much later that night, at the end of my shift, my youngest child showed up in a taxi to pick me up instead of my husband.

"Hi Mom, have you talked to Dad? He never picked me up from work so I had to get a cab. I knew you didn't have a way home either. I've been calling him but he's not answering. Something must be wrong," my son said as I joined him in the backseat.

"Never picked you up?" my stomach sank as I pondered what might have gone wrong.

"No wonder he's not answering," I thought, as we approached a car wreck at the stop light at our exit. My son got out of the cab as it came to a stop. I was unable to speak or move. I just felt numb and lightheaded.

"It's not him," my son said, seeming almost

disappointed as he got back into the cab. "Where is he? This is so strange," my son said with fear in his eyes. I didn't have the answers. I didn't know what to do with all the images coming to mind in waves of dread. Something terrible had happened.

We spent the remainder of that night in mental anguish, as I could not even gather the strength to breathe, let alone sleep. Even with all that we'd been through in our marriage, this was so unlike Greg. I called a friend to ask what I should do. It never dawned on me to call family. As if programmed, I was in a mode of protecting any potential indiscretions involving my children or him. My friend suggested calling hospitals and jails. *What is even happening to my life right now?* I thought, fretting over the possibilities.

"GOD PLEASE HELP ME BREATHE!" I cried. I literally struggled to breathe. I kept checking my phone, hoping I had missed his call even though I never heard it ring. The terror was causing my central nervous system to malfunction. I finally drifted off into a light slumber from sheer exhaustion.

Early that next morning, the phone rang. I have never been so anxious and afraid to answer a phone in my life.

"Dallas Correctional Facility calling, would you accept a collect call from inmate Gregory Sargent?"

My husband informed me he had spent the night

in detox and he was in jail, charged with driving under the influence. Of all the possible emotions, I mostly felt betrayed. How could he let this happen? Why NOW? The betrayal I felt had to make room for the anger. I was seething. I don't remember anything else he said. I immediately gathered every ounce of liquor we had in the cupboard and poured it down the drain.

That was the moment I realized I was in this by myself. I was in this miserable hotel room, in this miserable marriage, with this miserable job with this man who was able to be quite happy in my misery. It only got worse from there. I was trying to believe in something that would never exist, the possibility of a stable home and a coming together of intention. He had totaled our only car, and now we were faced with the expense of a DWI.

We had agreed on doing whatever was necessary to stay on our feet financially. But this setback was too big of a hurdle to come back from. I was unable to believe that we could turn things around. Mentally, I checked out. I stopped asking, WHY and started asking, WHAT is the lesson to be learned here? I once heard someone say, "Never wait on something bad to turn good."

Finally, after 30 years, I had the courage to abandon this sinking ship. The lessons about myself were invaluable, however painful the learning.

The Appointment

SHERRAIN MYLES

"When adversity comes, show up with your grown up."

Growing up, I watched you make hard decisions. You were always decisive and determined. I saw your strength as a trailblazing banker and entrepreneur. I witnessed your bravery as you reinvented yourself again and again. You never quit. It was as if quitting defied your very being. Only recently have I realized that your strength and determination are the greatest I've ever known. I am hoping I will find *you* in *me* right now, when I need it most.

It's early March and it's your first visit with this physician. My thoughts are scattered as I rush through the house to make sure that I have everything that you will need for him to best understand your diagnosis. I thought parenthood was a beast, but being the adult grandchild to an already established, now mostly cantankerous, but always determined to have her way, grandmother, makes even the most difficult childrearing seem easy. My gut reminds me that this will be a difficult appointment. So, it's my responsibility to do as you always told me and be that "big girl you know I am." Damn, I wish that big girl would show up.

I pull into the parking lot. I have second thoughts about agreeing to the onsite transportation bringing you, instead of picking you up myself. These last few days you've been quiet—a different kind of agreeable that I've never seen before. I hadn't stopped to consider what might be going on in your head. You've always been the one with the answers; the one who challenged me to face anything difficult head on; the one reminding me to never let my doubts or self-defined weaknesses get in the way. My life's assignment is to remember that although failure happens, failing myself is not acceptable. Still, I don't feel properly trained to be the emotional and physical support for the two of us. This is an exam that I'm not ready to take.

I called Momma last night to see how she was with everything. Since moving you to the metroplex with me, it's been less stressful for her, but I know she's concerned about the information we received from your last doctor's visit. She and I talked about how your disposition has changed and she offered me the watered-down version of your expectations.

The non-emergency transport vehicle pulls up and I quickly collect myself and your things. I take a deep breath and put on my signature smile. It's what I watched you wear any time you were certain that the news would be something other than what you'd hoped for. I quickly open my car door and grab my bag with your insurance cards, medication lists, notes from previous appointments and the questions that I'd gone over with Mom last night. This is me, being the you that I'd seen so often when I was growing up. Before turning to make my way to the truck, I inhale deeply once more, hoping to gain positive energy for my greeting—because I don't know how you are feeling about today.

I walk toward the side of the vehicle where you are strapped tightly in the wheelchair. You grimace as the driver gently disconnects the latch to the support device that holds you in. Our eyes meet and the sides of your mouth turn up. Your face offers both relief and happiness when you see me. The driver asks me to sign a document releasing you into my care. It is in this moment that I really feel like your caregiver. How did we get here? You had always been the caregiver. You took care of everybody and everything! I always believed you held all of the answers, like a vault with the code that only recognized your fingerprints.

"Ma'am?" the driver asks.

"Oh, yes, here you go. No need for a return pickup, I'll bring her back," I say with an authority that I don't feel, returning his clipboard.

I glance at your face, smiling with approval, and the big girl takes over, assuming her position. It's showtime, she says. She feels like an imposter to me, but I am glad she's here.

"Hey Nanie!" I greet you as I lean over to kiss your cheek.

"Hey Rain!" you offer, smiling back. "I'm happy to see you, baby."

I wink at you, place my bag in your lap and take the reins as we start a journey that is both a beginning and an end.

We enter the first automatic sliding doors and stop to wait for the second set to open. The look of uncertainty on your face mirrors mine as we scan the waiting room to identify the next steps of our mission. Sitting at the desk to our right is a tall, thin lady with round tortoise shell glasses and disheveled red hair held loosely together with a paisley scrunchy. She has a warm smile with a demeanor to match. I push the wheelchair in her direction.

"Hello there," she says in a soft but raspy voice. "Do you have an appointment today?"

"Yes, ma'am," I reply. "Our appointment, or my grandmother's appointment, is with Dr. Grisham at 3:30. Her name is Mary Chaney."

"I see it here—yes. Do you have her insurance card and identification?" she asks, holding out her hand towards me to collect the items.

I look at you and see that you seem to have a calmness about the situation that lets me know you trust that I have all of this under control. Your gaze turns towards a nearby window. I wonder what you are thinking; wonder if the steps I've taken up to this point offer green checks or red x's on the caregiver test I feel like I'm taking. If the eyes are the windows to the soul, you must have your blinds shut!

I give the red-haired receptionist our information and watch as she slips each card into a reader. I remember the stories you told me about your daddy and your last time with him at the hospital. That time when you were his caregiver. I never asked how taking care of him made you feel. Maybe, you felt like me. Nah, you have always had the answers.

The receptionist returns the cards to me. I hand them to you and push you to the most convenient place for us to park and sit, careful not to bump you into anything.

"You trying to be a good driver today, huh?" you joke with that sly half-smile I know so well.

"I'm getting better," I respond, with the same

half-smile that would confirm to anyone that we are closely related.

Now seated next to you, with my small Bible of Nanie open to the pages that provide the answers to the fill-in-the-blank questions I've been given to complete, I look over at you. Your face is beaming with what I believe to be pride. Your eyes are sparkly and your smile so gracious. I also detect the hope for some unexpected, miraculous news. Something to erase what other physicians have already told us.

"Thank you for taking care of my appointments and my things, Rain. I sure do love you for all you do," you say, reaching over to pat my leg.

"You don't have to thank me, Nanie. You never have to thank me for anything I do for you. You're my Nanie!" I say with a big smile, trying hard to keep the flood of waiting tears from spilling over.

Big Girl barges into my moment:

Get it together, Sherrain! She needs you to be the freaking grown-up that she's shown you how to be...RIGHT NOW! Your red nose, hell, your whole damn expression—is something that she knows better than you do. Do not lose it. This is not the time. Pull. It. Together!

I quickly look away, place the paperwork on your lap, force a smile and lie about needing to use the restroom.

"I'll be right back, Nanie," I say, rushing out of your sight.

I'm not even sure I am going in the right direction, but my pace suggests I have an idea. I reach a long hallway with vending machines and decide to stop and gather myself. Gazing at the various colors and labels in the machine, I begin to wonder if the Big Girl was ever really a thing. Maybe it's always been some Jedi mind trick that you played on me to build me up. I suppose when I was younger, being your big girl meant sitting quietly in church just long enough to earn a Brach's Star Bright Peppermint from your purse. Maybe it worked more often than it didn't. Maybe I'm just not big enough for *this*. This thought, yep, this is the one that gives the tears permission to roll. Right now, I'm feeling like the Big Girl is only as real as Santa Clause and the Tooth Fairy. I feel like I'm failing.

I walk into the restroom to check my face in the mirror over the sink. I gather myself and look for the big girl's reflection, even if she is an imposter. I force a smile. You are waiting and I have to show up right. Just as I return to you, I hear your name.

"Mrs. Chaney?" someone calls from a door near the receptionist's desk.

"Nanie, that's us. Let's go." I gather up our belongings and grab the wheelchair handles.

We go through the door held open by a woman I later learn is Dr. Grisham's nurse. She leads us into a cold examination room with an exam table and two chairs. I sit in one and place my things in the other, wishing Momma was sitting beside me. The nurse takes your vitals and asks if you have any pain. She pulls a pain chart from her pocket with several faces representing varying pain levels. You point to the green smiling face and tell her you have no pain. She smiles, lets us know that the doctor will be in soon, then leaves the room.

We sit in silence. I don't know what to say. Our eyes connect and you smile. I smile back, wondering if your smile signifies a familiar feeling—one that you know, a feeling that can be comforted by something in your vault of answers. A knock on the door interrupts my thought. A small, dark-haired man with greenish eyes and a somewhat nervous smile enters the room and jams his hands into his pockets.

"Hello there, I'm Dr. Grisham," he says, extending one hand.

We both look up at him. He's not exactly what I expected, younger than I'd pictured. But he is supposed to be the best person to see for a second opinion.

"Good afternoon, Dr. Grisham. I'm Sherrain Myles and this is my grandmother, Mary Chaney," I reply.

"Hi-dee," you say in that greeting that I've never heard from anyone else but you.

"I've had an opportunity to look over the scans from your last physician, and I agree with the doctor's findings. The mass on your lungs is an aggressive lung cancer and it's in stage four."

Your look isn't one of defeat, or even disappointment, as you ask about chemotherapy and next steps. And you're back! It's like you have had enough, unbuckled your passenger-side seat belt, gotten out of the car, walked over to the driver's side and asked me to slide over so you can assume your position at the steering wheel. The woman who ascended be the first female, African American supervisor for M&P Bank and then launched a successful beauty salon business with her own funding, shows up and wants answers. And just as I am ready to relent and hand over the wheel, Dr. Grisham shifts his look to me and asks me to step outside with him.

"Mrs. Myles, your grandmother's condition should not be treated with chemo. Both her age and lack of life quality are my concern at this point. I'm not sure that it would even offer any more time. Do you understand?"

Words leave my mouth, but I am not sure what they are. My stomach is weak and I want my momma. I want anyone to deliver me from the task ahead. The doctor is leaving me to deliver this message to you and I don't want to take away your hope. I somehow find the strength to open the door. It seems so much heavier than it did when we walked in. Then I remember that I didn't open the door, the nurse did. I wonder if it was this heavy for her. My mind races, and I guess my gaze reflects my distance, because your voice snaps me out of my daydream.

"Rain? What'd he say?"

I don't have words yet—or even an idea of what I am supposed to do. I let go of the door and it slams, causing me to recognize that it *is* heavy—that it's not my imagination. I pray silently for God to appear and deliver what I've been charged with. But this is a prayer that He doesn't answer. It's only me, here with you and this prognosis. Three to six months. Hospice. That's all I remember from the doctor's message.

"He used all of the words that we didn't want to hear, Nanie," I say quietly. "Chemo is not an option."

My eyes well up, so I look away. Your eyes drift to your hands. I remember this look from the summer of 1988, when I'd gone with you to a doctor's appointment for my grandfather. I remember you telling me how important this visit with his doctor would be. Cecil had been unusually forgetful, and you'd had a hunch that it was more than just aging. Just before he was diagnosed with Alzheimer's, the hopeful smile appeared, then transitioned to the *I understand, but I wish it were better news,* smile.

This was a difficult appointment. I came with

the hope that a different reality would meet us here. But it hasn't. I help you out of the wheelchair and strap you into the car. I ask if you are comfortable, and you nod your head yes. Now sitting with this information—your own health status, you maintain your composure. I look at you and it hits me as I recognize our matching smiles. I will step up because I have to, because you've raised me for this moment. You've given me the understanding that although adversity comes, show up with your grown up, because failing you and failing myself is not an option.

About the Contributors

Inge Ford ~ We Are Seeds

Inge knows we all have stories to share. And, like many, she has struggled with getting words to paper. She delights in exploring ancestral teachings and merging new ideas relevant to our space and time. As a dentist, educator, activist, and mother, her global travels reinforce her belief that our narratives are important. The *Stories Are Medicine* Story Group was the catalyst needed to translate a momentous experience into an auspicious debut. She hails from Texas, and in true colloquial vernacular says, "Write that story, y'all."

Kimberly Bady ~ The Bittersweet Goodbye

Kim has been a leader for women in the areas of personal and spiritual development for over 20

years. She's led retreats, conferences and created rites of passage programs for teens and women of all ages. A registered yoga teacher and a Certified Holistic Health Coach, Kim uses her medicine of movement, writing, storytelling, dancing and teaching to inspire women in the courses she leads and the community she created, the Healthy Living, Healthy Aging Community. To learn more about Kim and her programs, visit shewellnesscoach.com.

Katherine Johnson ~ Woman Interrupted

A wife, mother of four, and grandmother of eight,

Katherine embraces and takes pride in her role as the matriarch of her family. She models what it truly means to cover your family in prayer, something she learned from her own mother before her passing. Katherine's nurturing extends beyond her family and loved ones to the elderly she works with as a private-duty caregiver and her work in ministry as a Staff Pastor. Katherine also owns her own personal accessories business, Kathy's Bling Shop and can be found praying for customers during her live online broadcasts.

Delois Butler ~ With God's Grace

Delois is a professional hair cutter, who just retired from Southwest Airlines after twenty-five years of employment as a Customer Service Agent. She is a mother of four children and a grandmother of seven beautiful grandchildren. Her dream had always been to write a book about her life's journey in order to help others, and this experience was a dream come true. She says, "When I was offered this opportunity, I am so glad I accepted it."

Julie Jones-Butler ~ The Birthday Party

Julie grew up in Louisiana. She is a beloved daughter of God, wife, mother, Pastor's wife and an entrepreneur. She and her husband, Jimmy, live in Texas with their beloved son. Julie has a BS in Biblical Counseling in Religious Studies from GMOR (Gospel Ministry Out Reach). Before taking the big leap of faith in writing, she always loved reading as a child, which influenced her interest in writing her

stories and her truths. She says that this writing experience has been fulfilling and has allowed her to heal on different levels of her personal and professional life. She believes that when you write your stories, goals and truths on paper, they will come to pass, and that writing truly is medicine to your soul.

Koinonia I. Martin-Page ~ Altar Call

Koinonia first learned the power of sharing our stories from her mother during testimony service in the Black Church tradition. She credits that power with helping her to forge her path from her

beginnings as a Head Start program student to being a first-generation college graduate of the Ivy League. She has gone on to use her skills to advocate and build community, as a licensed attorney, attorney-broker, philanthropist, and public servant. She most cherishes spending time with her three sons, Jesse, Zachary, and Jude, and her husband, Ben.

CYNTARA SANDERS ~ Through the Eyes of the Little Girl

Cyntara has known for years there was so much she wanted to write about that would help awaken and heal the world. And right when she no longer cared what others thought, the opportunity to begin writing showed up. Writing about her childhood trauma has opened up the teacher within. She currently teaches Naturopathic Reiki and she looks forward to writing many more books and Master classes. She is a proud native Houstonian and mother of two adult children.

DEMITRI SARGENT ~ Three Days, Three Months, Thirty Years

From surviving to thriving has been is Demitri's mantra. She says, as she lives through the ebbs and flows of thriving, she is learning more about the power of her own voice. This writing experience has created the space for her to find her voice again and she hopes to share with others just how beautiful your life can be when living as your fully-expressed

self. Demitri looks forward to curating Soul Care events in the near future and sharing more healing stories with the world.

Sherrain Myles ~ The Appointment

Sherrain's most pertinent caregiving role outside of parenting was being the primary caregiver for her ailing grandmother. While Sherrain has a successful career in healthcare sales, and has dedicated her

time and efforts to assisting vulnerable family members and their support systems with obtaining the appropriate level of care, professional experiences had not prepared her for the personal journey of caregiving. In *The Appointment*, readers are given a candid glimpse into the abrupt changes that occur during caregiving. Sherrain received a Bachelor of Arts from Southeastern Oklahoma State University in Durant, Oklahoma and is a native of Denison, Texas. She is a member of Sigma Gamma Rho Sorority, Inc and resides in Grand Prairie, Texas with her husband, daughter, and son.

Gina Carroll ~ Editor

Gina describes herself as a story wrangler and writing evangelist. As a writing coach, editor and author of *A Story That Matters: A Gratifying Approach to Writing About Your Life*, she helps aspiring writers and business professionals get their life stories in print. For her, the *Stories Are Medicine* Story Group is as deeply meaningful and rewarding personally as it is professionally.

Acknowledgments

The Stories Are Medicine experience has been as much a gift to Kim Bady and me as it has the participants. Each writer committed to be fully "in"—to work and learn, but most of all, to show up. Showing up for the group and for themselves is why this book exists. And I want to acknowledge every single writer, who had to fight through her busy life. She had to decide every single week that even though she had a trillion things to do, she would carve out this time; throw on some lipstick (or not, talking about myself here); login, and take part. And when she did, we were all deeply grateful that she came to take her place and give of herself for that hour and a half.

So thank you, Cyntara, Koinonia, Katherine,

Delois, Demetri, Sherrain, Julie, Inge and of course, Kim. Your stories changed us. Your feedback fed us. Your smiles and tears uplifted and inspired us. And I, for one, am so honored and grateful that I am now a tiny part of your story, that part about how and when you got serious about writing; that piece of your life story about when and how you became a published author. But most of all, that turning point when you looked inside, dealt with what you found and thereby, uncovered more of your dazzling light.

On behalf of our group, a heart-felt thank-you to the readers and supporters who graciously accepted our invitations to read and provide comments on our drafts—family, friends and trusted loved ones. You are special folk because you said yes and you provided the encouragement and the feedback so crucial to the process.

Thank you, as well, to Anita Bunkley, our book editor, for putting a shine to these stories and this manuscript, as a whole. Thank you for your willingness...and your patience!

Deep rivers of gratitude must to go out to Deborah Daly for taking us on and making our publishing dreams come true. We so appreciate all of your graciousness, enthusiasm and professional know-how.

Endless thanks to Danielle Boodoo-Fortune for the gorgeous art that graces our cover. She was the first artist who we featured during our very first session, and her works stuck with us. We dreamed big with the thought of her art becoming a part of our book. And here we are! Here she is! We are so grateful and inspired.

Contributor Credits

Made in the USA
Monee, IL
17 June 2022

98181559R00069